Gold EXPERIENCE

A2
Key for Schools

Vocabulary
and Grammar
Workbook

Kathryn Alevizos

Contents

01	Enjoy yourself	4
02	Can't live without it?	10
Revision Units 1 – 2		16
03	We ♥ school	18
04	What a bargain!	24
Revision Units 3 – 4		30
05	Mysteries from history	32
06	Have a good trip!	38
Revision Units 5 – 6		44
07	You can do it!	46
08	See the world	52
Revision Units 7 – 8		58
09	Let me entertain you	60
10	Eat well, feel well	66
Revision Units 9 – 10		72
11	More than a job	74
12	Summer fun!	80
Revision Units 11 – 12		86
Exam information		88

Enjoy yourself

READING

1 Read the article and complete the table with information about the two teenagers.

We love cooking

Isabella Bliss and Georgia Bradford have the same hobby: they love cooking. The two teenagers are both winners of the TV show *Junior Masterchef*. Isabella is a winner of the show in Australia and Georgia is a winner of the show in the UK.

Isabella is from Brisbane in Australia. She is always in the kitchen with her twin sister Sofia. Sofia also loves cooking and likes entering competitions. Isabella's mother is Italian and her favourite food is Italian food. Isabella wants to open a restaurant with her sister in the future. They want to call the restaurant Is-Sofia. The twin sisters also have a cookbook. It's called *A Little Bit of This, a Little Bit of That*.

Georgia is from Leigh-on-Sea in England. She loves being in the kitchen. She lives with her parents and her two sisters. She often cooks for her family at home. Georgia's favourite food is fish. She wants to be a chef in the future. Her other hobby is horse-riding. Her dream is to have a family house with horses and a restaurant in Cornwall. Georgia also wants to cook Italian food in her restaurant.

Family name	First name	Town	Country
1) _Bliss_	2)	3)	4) ....
5)	6)	7)	8) ....

2 Read the article again. Choose right (R), wrong (W) or doesn't say (DS) for each sentence.

1 Isabella and Georgia are winners of *Junior Masterchef*. _R_
2 Isabella and Georgia are the same age. ....
3 Isabella's mother and father are from Australia. ....
4 Isabella and her sister want to work together. ....
5 Georgia's sisters love cooking. ....
6 Cooking is Georgia's only hobby. ....

VOCABULARY
Hobbies and Leisure

1 Match the hobbies with the pictures.

cooking   ~~dancing~~   drawing   fishing
reading   singing

1 _dancing_   2 ....
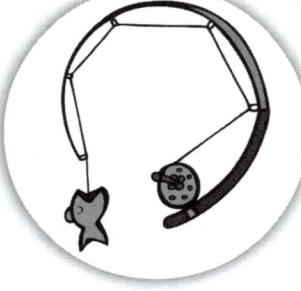 

3 ....   4 ....

5 ....   6 ....

01 Enjoy yourself

2 Complete the sentences with these words.

> ~~cooking~~   dance   fishing   painting
> read   sing

1 Do you like _cooking_ ?
   Yes, I make really good spaghetti bolognese!
2 Do you always .... a book before you go to bed?
   Yes, every night.
3 Do your parents .... ?
   My mum does. She has a nice voice, but my dad doesn't.
4 Do you do .... in your art class?
   Yes and we do drawing.
5 Does Stephanie .... ?
   Yes, she does ballet.
6 Do you go .... with your granddad in his boat?
   Yes, and we cook what we catch when we get back.

3 Choose the correct words.

1 Martin loves *cook/cooking*. He makes great chocolate cakes.
2 Francesca goes *fishes/fishing* with her dad and brother every Sunday.
3 Caroline and Maisy *playing/play* in a rock band.
4 We usually *draw/drawing* animals or people in our art class.
5 They enjoy *read/reading* comics.
6 Do you like *sing/singing*?
7 I *cook/cooking* breakfast for my family every Saturday.
8 My brother's not very good at *paint/painting*.

4 Find and write four things you can play and three things you can watch.

c	h	f	y	t	r	f	r	e	d	n	f	i
l	o	k	j	u	h	g	f	d	e	e	s	k
i	o	m	u	s	l	i	g	v	n	g	f	e
l	b	h	p	o	o	n	u	n	e	i	t	u
k	v	y	i	u	f	t	i	u	n	i	b	d
e	h	u	a	t	t	e	t	e	n	d	v	d
m	k	o	n	o	n	e	a	n	g	l	i	o
t	u	i	o	n	f	d	r	c	n	f	m	x
v	n	t	r	e	e	r	i	g	d	i	n	t
o	e	m	b	t	i	g	e	e	a	l	b	i
t	n	c	h	e	s	s	n	o	n	m	l	n
e	v	i	n	u	s	k	o	n	e	k	e	k
d	i	p	o	j	d	e	o	g	r	e	a	s

Things you can play
1 _piano_
2 ....
3 ....
4 ....

Things you can watch
1 ....
2 ....
3 ....

5 Match the meanings (1–6) with the words (a–f).

1 the sounds you make playing instruments or singing
2 something that you post without an envelope
3 a small piece of paper you buy and stick onto a letter
4 an overnight visit to another person's home
5 you watch films in this building
6 a magazine with stories and pictures

a stamp
b comic
c cinema
d music
e postcard
f sleepover

6 Choose the correct verbs.

1 *watch/collect* comics
2 *play/go* on a sleepover
3 *watch/go* a TV programme
4 *watch/go* to the cinema
5 *listen/collect* to music
6 *play/watch* the violin
7 *watch/go* shopping
8 *listen/collect* stamps

5

7 Match the sentences (1–8) with the sentences (A–H).
1 I love reading comics. _G_
2 Suzie and Rachel are good at football. ___
3 Ricky hates shopping. ___
4 I'm OK at drawing. ___
5 We don't like going to the cinema. ___
6 William's brilliant at chess. ___
7 My dad isn't good at singing. ___
8 Gina's got an amazing collection of postcards. ___

A He's got a terrible voice!
B He's always winning competitions.
C I prefer painting.
D They play for the school team.
E She's got 500!
F He thinks it's boring.
G My favourite is called _Demo_.
H We like watching DVDs at home.

8 Complete the text with the best answer, A, B or C, for each space.

My friends and I all 1) _have_ different hobbies. I love singing and 2) ___ to my MP3 player. We all enjoy going to the 3) ___ together. Sometimes we watch a 4) ___ at someone's house. My friend Lucy 5) ___ the piano. She's really good. I play the 6) ___ . My brother doesn't like listening to me! He usually stays in his room and plays 7) ___ .

1 A take   (B) have   C make
2 A listening   B watching   C playing
3 A film   B sleepover   C cinema
4 A TV   B DVD   C computer games
5 A plays   B does   C makes
6 A shopping   B violin   C drawing
7 A MP3 player   B comics   C computer games

GRAMMAR
Present simple

1 Choose the correct words.
1 Oliver _plays/play_ the guitar and the piano.
2 Melissa and Ruby _goes/go_ shopping every Saturday.
3 He _don't/doesn't_ have a hobby.
4 _Does/Do_ they listen to music in the car?
5 We _doesn't/don't_ like painting.
6 The children _watch/watches_ TV after school.
7 She _take/takes_ amazing photographs.
8 I _doesn't/don't_ go to the cinema with my family.

2 Complete the letter with the present simple form of the verbs in brackets.

Hi, Tom

Summer camp 1) _is_ (be) brilliant! We 2) ___ (do) lots of different activities here. In the morning we play games. Sometimes I 3) ___ (play) chess and sometimes I do sport outside. In the afternoon we do art and music. I 4) ___ (like) painting and drawing. My brother 5) ___ (enjoy) the music classes here. He 6) ___ (love) playing the guitar. In the evenings we often 7) ___ (watch) a film together or play computer games. It 8) ___ (be) great fun!

See you soon,

Jacob

3 Complete these questions with the verbs in brackets and _do_ or _does_.
1 _Do_ you _have_ (have) a hobby?
2 ___ she ___ (like) music?
3 ___ they ___ (enjoy) taking photos?
4 ___ we ___ (start) our painting class today?
5 ___ Liam ___ (collect) anything?
6 ___ I ___ (buy) my ticket for the dance show here?
7 ___ your teacher ___ (sing)?

4 Match the questions (1–6) with the answers (A–F).

1 Do you go shopping with your parents? _D_
2 Does your sister go to a chess club? ......
3 Do Ben and Karen do painting at school? ......
4 Do they go to the cinema? ......
5 Does Matthew collect anything? ......
6 Does Jane play the piano or the guitar? ......

A Yes, she does. She goes to a club at school.
B Yes, they love films.
C Yes, he does. He's got 600 stamps.
D Yes, I do. We go every Saturday.
E No, she doesn't. She doesn't like music.
F No, they don't. They only do drawing.

Adverbs of frequency

5 Put the words in the correct place.

~~always~~   never   not often   not usually
often   sometimes

1 _always_ — 100%
2 ......
3 ......
4 ......
5 ......
6 ...... — 0%

6 Put the words in the correct order to make sentences.

1 TV / usually / in the evening / My parents / watch / .
My parents usually watch TV in the evening.

2 go / often / in the holidays / shopping / We / .
......

3 in June / There / sometimes / is / a chess competition / .
......

4 Kiera / never / her music lessons / enjoys / .
......

5 read / Jasmine / usually / comics / doesn't / .
......

6 always / My singing lessons / fun / are / .
......

7 don't / They / go / on sleepovers / often / .
......

7 Look at the information about Amy and Jonathan and write sentences.

	Amy	Jonathan
play computer games	often	not usually
go on a sleepover	sometimes	never
take photographs	not often	often
sing in the bathroom	not usually	always

1 Amy / play computer games
Amy often plays computer games.

2 Jonathan / play computer games
......

3 Amy / go on a sleepover
......

4 Jonathan / go on a sleepover
......

5 Amy / take photographs
......

6 Jonathan / take photographs
......

7 Amy / sing in the bathroom
......

8 Jonathan / sing in the bathroom
......

LISTENING

1 🔊 **1.1 Listen to Simon talking to his dad about his friends' hobbies. Which of these hobbies does Simon not talk about?**

Simon does not talk about 1) _____ and 2) _____ .

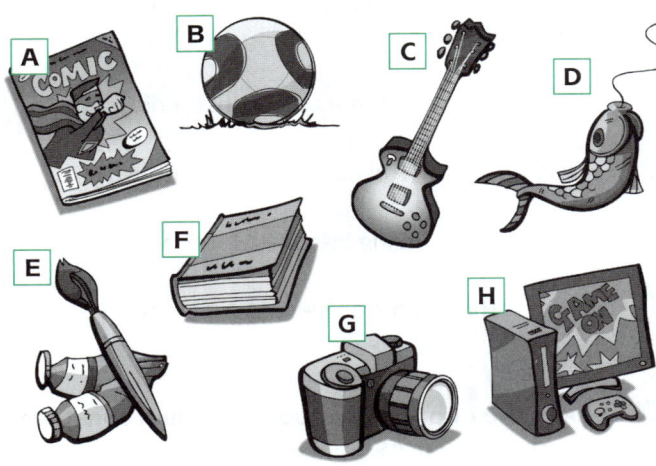

2 🔊 **1.2 Listen again and complete the notes.**

Simon's friends' hobbies

Jack: loves 1) *fishing*
Helen: loves taking 2) _____
Pete: interested in 3) _____
Tom: collects 4) _____
Sarah: loves playing 5) _____ games
Jon: plays the 6) _____

GRAMMAR
many/much

1 Complete the table with these words.

~~books~~ friends fun hobbies money music people time

much	many
	books

2 Complete the dialogues with *much* or *many*.

1. How *many* musical instruments do you play?
   — Two – the piano and the violin.

2. Have you got _____ music on your MP3 player?
   — Yeah, I've got about 300 songs on it.

3. How _____ people go to the chess club?
   — About twelve.

4. Do you have _____ free time?
   — Not after school, but I do at weekends.

5. I want a new hobby, but I don't have _____ money.
   — My hobby's singing. It's free.

SPEAKING SKILLS

1 Choose the correct answer.

1. What sport *do you like*/does you like/like you?
2. *What*/Who/When do you play football?
3. Is Anna/Anna do/*Does Anna* good at dancing?
4. Where play/*do you play*/you play chess?
5. Does your brother enjoying/enjoy/*enjoys* singing?
6. Where does you like/you likes/*do you like* to read?

2 Choose the correct answer, A, B or C.

1. Do you like cooking?
   A Not really. I think it's brilliant.
   B Yes, but I'm not very good at it.
   C Yes, I hate it!
2. Is Lilly good at drawing?
   A Yes, she does.
   B Yes, she's brilliant!
   C Yes, she draws.
3. When do you like listening to music?
   A In the evenings.
   B Sometimes.
   C Rock and pop music.
4. Do you like going to the cinema?
   A Yes, I like the weekends.
   B Yes, I like my friends.
   C Yes, I like American films.
5. How often do you go shopping?
   A Every Saturday morning.
   B With my best friend.
   C I usually buy clothes and shoes.
6. Do you collect anything?
   A I go to chess club.
   B Fishing and football.
   C Baseball caps. I've got eighty-six.

WRITING

1 Put the words in the correct order.

1. you / to the chess club / with me / to go / ? / Do / want
   Do you want to go to the chess club with me?
2. . / every / after school / Monday / It's
   ....
3. in / It's / 11A / . / Room
   ....
4. starts / It / at 3.45 / at 3.00 / and / . / finishes
   ....
5. good / It's / . / fun
   ....
6. / do / you / ? / think / What
   ....

2 Complete the email with these words.

do   library   want   Hi   take   starts

1) *Hi* Ben,

Do you 2) .... to go to the photography club? It 3) .... tomorrow after school. We meet in the 4) .... at 4 p.m. We go to different places to 5) .... photos. It's really good. What 6) .... you think?

Mark

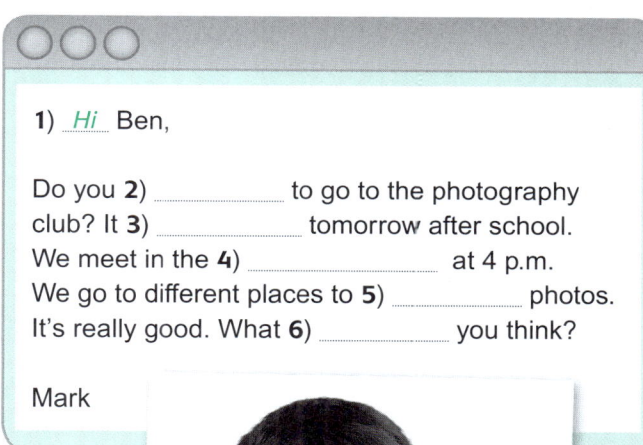

3 Write an email to a friend. Invite him/her to your tennis club. Tell him/her the time, day and place the club meets. Remember to start and finish in a friendly way.

02 Can't live without it?

READING

1 Read the report and choose the correct answer, A, B or C.

Teach your granny to text
a report by Alexander Zelenko

My class at school is reading an English book called *Teach Your Granny to Text and Other Ways to Change the World*. It's a book about simple everyday actions you can do to change the world. The book's message is that 'small actions x lots of people = big change'. Our class is trying to do action 15: teach your granny to text. The idea is not only to teach grandmas, but to help anyone use modern technology. This week, everyone in our class is teaching someone they know how to use some technology. Some students are teaching their grandparents to text. Other students are teaching their parents to download music. Every day, the students write about what they are doing in their school diary. Here's what some of the students are doing.

Rosalie, 14
'I'm teaching my grandma to use her mobile phone. She is eighty-two this year. She's a very good student! She now knows how to send texts from her phone, but it takes her about five minutes! I want to teach her to use the camera on her phone next.'

Lucas, 15
'I'm not teaching my grandma to text. She sends texts all the time – and she's got a really cool phone! I'm teaching my grandpa to use the Internet. My grandpa loves gardening. I'm teaching him to use gardening websites.'

Harriet, 14
'I'm teaching my dad to download music and films on his phone. My dad's got a really good phone, but he only uses it to make phone calls. I'm showing him all the other things his phone does.'

1 What are the students at this school doing?
  A They're sending texts to their grandmas.
  B They're teaching people to use modern technology.
  C They're learning about mobile phones and the Internet.

2 Where did the students get the idea for the school project?
  A From a book.
  B From a film.
  C From their teacher.

3 Where are the students writing about the project?
  A On their laptops.
  B On the school website.
  C In their school diaries.

4 What does Rosalie want to teach her grandma next?
  A How to download music.
  B How to email.
  C How to take photos.

5 Why isn't Lucas teaching his grandma to text?
  A She knows how to text.
  B She doesn't have a mobile phone.
  C She isn't interested in mobile phones.

6 What is Harriet showing her dad?
  A How to choose a good phone.
  B How to use his mobile in different ways.
  C How to make phone calls on his mobile.

2 Find words in the report that match the meanings and complete the table.

Meaning	Word
not difficult	1) s*imple*
the important idea of a book, film, etc.	2) m
using new ideas, not old	3) m
copy music or other information from the Internet	4) d
good or fashionable	5) c

VOCABULARY
Technology

1 Complete the crossword.

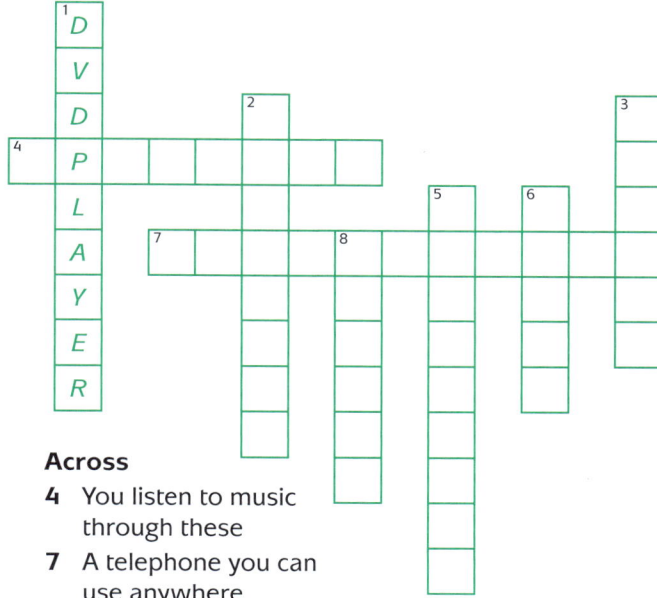

Across
4 You listen to music through these
7 A telephone you can use anywhere

Down
1 You watch DVDs on this
2 The part of a computer you use to type words
3 The part of a computer you look at to read information
5 A small gadget for listening to music
6 Something you use to move around the screen of a computer
8 A small computer that you can move easily

2 Choose the correct words.
1 Can we watch the film at your house?
   Sorry, my brother's using the computer and our *MP3 player/DVD player* isn't working.
2 Don't eat your lunch at the computer! You're dropping food on the *keyboard/screen*.
3 Rachel, your dinner's on the table. Put your *speakers/mobile phone* down, please.
   OK, but can I send one quick text to Emma?
4 Can you play music on your laptop?
   Yes, but the *keyboard/speakers* aren't very good so the music's not very loud.
5 Why are you closing the curtains?
   The sun's shining on my laptop and I can't read the information on the *screen/MP3 player*.
6 How do I open this file?
   Move the arrow on top of it and then click the button on the *speakers/mouse*.

3 Match the sentence beginnings (1–6) with the endings (A–F).
1 Oscar is sending *F*
2 Olivia and Sophia surf ___
3 I'm listening to music with ___
4 Every Sunday Nathan chats ___
5 It's cheap and easy to download ___
6 They're looking at ___

A my headphones.
B music.
C online with his cousins in Venezuela.
D a website about street dancing.
E the Internet together in the evenings.
F an email to his teacher about his homework.

4 Complete the sentences with these words.

> download   email   headphones   ~~online~~
> surfing   texts   webcam

1 Nicky likes chatting to her friends *online* .
2 Dean and Andrew ___ all their music.
3 I enjoy ___ the Internet in the evening.
4 Rebecca sends lots of ___ with her new phone.
5 I listen to music with my ___ on the bus.
6 They're sending a long ___ to their friends in France.
7 Our grandparents in Australia can see us with our new ___ .

5 Choose the best answer, A, B or C.
1 Look at this new *gadget* . It tells you the time and it is a torch and an MP3 player.
   A gadget   B camcorder   C Xbox
2 This ___ is amazing! It walks and talks.
   A watch   B robot   C laptop
3 I'm making a film of our family with my new ___ .
   A camcorder   B Xbox   C robot
4 Do you like my new ___ ? It shows what time it is in ten different countries.
   A mouse   B webcam   C watch
5 My mum's new ___ is really cool. She's reading something on it now.
   A keyboard   B camcorder   C e-book
6 Michael and Poppy love playing on their ___ . They have lots of different games.
   A Xbox   B robot   C screen

6 Complete the text with these words.

computers   Internet   ~~laptop~~   mobile
online   reads   send   surf

How much technology does your family use?
My brother and I have a 1) _laptop_ each.
We often 2) _____ emails and 3) _____
the Internet. My granddad's got an e-book and he
4) _____ every day. My dad doesn't like
5) _____, but he does have a
6) _____ phone. He has to take it with him
to work. My mum doesn't have a laptop, but she
gets the 7) _____ on her phone. She loves
shopping 8) _____.

7 Complete the sentences with these words.

bored   ~~diary~~   entrance   experiments
great   hard

1 I write what I'm thinking about and feeling in my _diary_.
2 My new mobile phone is _____. I love it!
3 All my friends are busy and I've got nothing to do. I feel really _____.
4 You go into the building through the main _____.
5 We do lots of cool _____ in our science lessons.
6 This online maths test is very _____. I don't understand any of the questions.

8 Choose the correct words.

Hi Bart
You aren't answering your mobile 1) *phone*/*text* and I need your help! I hope you see this 2) *note*/*email* soon. I'm doing my homework on today's science 3) *entrance*/*experiment* and I can't find my notes. Can you 4) *send*/*write* me an email with the teacher's questions? I think all the answers are 5) *mobile*/*online*. Do you remember the 6) *website*/*Internet* we need to look at?
Thanks
Tom

GRAMMAR
Present continuous

1 Complete the table with the *-ing* form of the verbs.

ride	1)	_riding_
get	2)	
have	3)	
hit	4)	
make	5)	
win	6)	
drive	7)	
sit	8)	

2 Put the words in the correct order to make sentences.

1 some robots / are / Jack and Liam / looking at / .
   Jack and Liam are looking at some robots.
2 writing / Deborah / in her school diary / is / .
3 a science experiment / are / The students / doing / .
4 watching a film / am / on my laptop / I / .
5 Oscar / a photo / is / on his mobile / taking / .
6 about King Henry VIII / We / reading / are / on the Internet / .

3 Choose the correct words.

1 The DVD player *isn't*/*aren't* working.
2 James *is*/*are* waiting for us.
3 My parents *is*/*are* watching a film in the lounge.
4 Helen *aren't*/*isn't* feeling well.
5 The children *is*/*are* playing computer games.
6 It *aren't*/*isn't* raining now.
7 We *is*/*are* doing our homework.
8 Kiera *is*/*are* driving to the beach.
9 Olly and Fran *is*/*are* cooking spaghetti.
10 My sisters *isn't*/*aren't* having lunch at school today.

02 Can't live without it?

4 Complete the sentences with the present continuous form of the verbs in brackets. Use contractions when possible.

1 We _'re talking_ (talk) to my dad in Dubai.
2 Martin and Noah _____ (play) a computer game.
3 They _____ (download) a film from the Internet.
4 I _____ (text) my friend Suzanna.
5 Carl _____ (write) his English essay on his laptop.
6 Marie and Didier _____ (look) for a good music website.
7 You _____ (send) a lot of texts to your friend.
8 I _____ (make) a short film with my camcorder.

5 Complete the sentences about Ella's family. Use these words and use contractions when possible.

> eat / a cake   read / a book
> sleep / on the rug   talk / on the phone
> ~~watch / TV~~   work / on a laptop

1 Ella _____'s watching TV._
2 Charlie _____
3 Ella's mum _____
4 Ella's dad _____
5 Ella's grandma _____
6 Ella's dog and cat _____

LISTENING

1 🔊 2.1 Listen to a man on the radio talking about a mobile phone exhibition. Complete the table.

Name of exhibition:	1) A _history_ of mobile phones
Number of phones in exhibition:	2) _____
Phones from the years:	3) _____ to 2015
Exhibition ends:	4) 20th _____
Cost for students:	5) £ _____

2 🔊 2.2 Listen again and choose the correct answers.

1 It is the *second/first* day of the exhibition.
2 The man speaks to some students at the *museum/their* school.
3 The students are having a *science/technology* lesson.
4 The students think the exhibition is *boring/interesting*.
5 The man's favourite mobile phone at the exhibition is from *1988/1987*.
6 He says the phone is big and *ugly/heavy*.

GRAMMAR
Present continuous and present simple

1 Choose the best answer, A, B or C.

1 My dad usually drives us to school, but today we _are taking_ the bus.
   A take   **B** are taking   C is taking
2 Mr Pritchard _____ us today because our teacher is ill.
   A is teaching   B teach   C teaches
3 _____ to his MP3 player at the moment?
   A Are Robbie listening   B Does Robbie listen
   C Is Robbie listening
4 Henry _____ football today. He's not feeling very well.
   A doesn't play   B isn't playing
   C not playing
5 Every year we _____ to a music festival with my cousins.
   A go   B are going   C goes
6 Look, Jack's over there. He _____ his lunch with his friends.
   A is having   B are having   C has

2 Complete the email with the present simple or present continuous form of the verbs in brackets. Use contractions when possible.

Hi Kiera
How are you? Are you having a good holiday? I 1) _'m staying_ (stay) at my grandparents' house for the holidays. They 2) _____ (live) in the mountains. It's an amazing place. There 3) _____ (be) lots of things to do here. Every day we 4) _____ (go) fishing or horse-riding. It's great fun. I can't phone you because there 5) _____ (not be) a signal for my mobile phone at my grandparents' house. I 6) _____ (write) this email in an Internet café in town. My grandparents 7) _____ (do) some shopping.
I hope you 8) _____ (have) a good time.
See you next week!
Jennie

3 Complete the conversation between Laura and her friend, Paul, with one word in each space.

Laura
Are 1) _you_ going home now?

Paul
No, I'm 2) _____ to my cousin's house. I 3) _____ staying with him at the moment.

Laura
Really? Why?

Paul
My parents 4) _____ doing some work in the house. There's no electricity so the Internet 5) _____ working. I'm using my cousin's computer for my homework.

Laura
Where 6) _____ your sister staying?

Paul
She's at my cousin's house, too. It 7) _____ a really big house so there 8) _____ a bedroom for me and my sister.

02 Can't live without it?

SPEAKING SKILLS

1 Look at the pictures and complete the sentences with these words.

> opposite   between   in front of
> next to   ~~behind~~

1 The girl is standing _behind_ the tree.
2 The girl is standing _____ the boy.
3 The girl is standing _____ the table.
4 The girl is standing _____ the boy and the tree.
5 The girl is sitting _____ the boy.

2 Tom is talking about a photo on his mobile phone. Look at the picture and complete the text with these words.

> in front of   between   opposite
> behind   ~~next to~~

"This is a picture of my friends and me. We're at Mark's birthday party. I'm the boy with black hair. I'm sitting 1) _next to_ Sara. She's got long blonde hair. Mark is standing 2) _____ me. He's wearing a silly party hat! The girl with short curly hair is my sister. She's sitting 3) _____ me. My best friend, Joe, is standing 4) _____ the window. The boy with blonde hair 5) _____ Joe and the door is Elliot. He's really funny!"

WRITING

1 Match the sentences.

1 I play on my Xbox with my sister after school. _D_
2 I take my iPod with me everywhere. ___
3 I've got 30 books on my e-book. ___
4 I love sending texts from my mobile phone. ___
5 My dad bought me my watch. ___
6 I love my camcorder. ___

A I send about 50 every day.
B I really enjoy making videos of my friends with it.
C I've got about 1,500 songs on it.
D We play the games on the TV in our bedroom.
E I never read paper books now.
F It tells the time and I can listen to music on it.

2 Choose the correct words.

My favourite gadget is my laptop. It's black 1) _and_/because/but pink. I love my laptop 2) and/but/because I can use it anywhere. It's got a webcam, 3) because/but/and I don't use it very much. I love chatting to my friends online 4) and/because/but looking at all my photos. I can't live without it!

3 Write about your favourite room in your house. Describe the room, explain why you like it and what you like doing there.

15

Revision Units 1 – 2

VOCABULARY

1 Choose the best answer, A, B or C.

1 I love _cooking_. I often make cakes with my mum.
   A drawing   B singing   **C cooking**
2 Harriet has a new _____ . She does her homework on it.
   A laptop   B camera   C screen
3 Every Friday, Jack goes to the _____ with his friends. He loves films.
   A sleepover   B cinema   C shopping
4 Freya loves looking at _____ about famous people.
   A webcams   B speakers   C websites
5 Charlie collects _____ . He's got about 500.
   A reading   B postcards   C shopping
6 My brother's got a new _____ . He reads it all the time.
   A e-book   B mobile   C camcorder

2 Complete Damien's description of his room with these words.

> comics   email   ~~laptop~~   listen   painting
> play   read   watch

Hi. My name's Damien and this is my bedroom. My favourite thing in my room is my 1) _laptop_ . I 2) _____ films, 3) _____ to music and 4) _____ my friends on it. I've also got a guitar, but I don't 5) _____ it very often. My hobby at the moment is 6) _____ . On my desk I've got all my brushes and paper. At the moment I'm doing a picture of my dog, Barney. I've got lots of books and 7) _____ in my room. I always 8) _____ before I go to bed. I'm reading a great book about robots at the moment.

3 Choose the correct words.

1 Can I use your _laptop/headphones_, please? I want to send an email to my sister.
   Yes, of course. Here you are.
2 Where's your sister?
   She's having a _singing/cooking_ lesson. She wants to be a pop star!
3 Do you know how to play _chess/the violin_?
   No, but my brother does. He loves music.
4 This website's great.
   Yeah, I know. I _download/surf_ all my music from it.
5 What are you watching?
   It's a _film/TV programme_ about tigers. It's on every day for half an hour.
6 I can't read my emails because the sun's shining on the computer _mouse/screen_.
   I can close the curtains for you.

4 Match the sentences (1–8) with the sentences (A–H).

1 Robert loves cooking. _F_
2 My mum's got a new mobile phone. ___
3 I always buy my clothes online. ___
4 My sister's good at playing the guitar. ___
5 Rachel never sends emails to her friends. ___
6 My dad and brother are fishing together. ___
7 My brother's not asleep. ___
8 Georgia often goes on a sleepover. ___

A She always sends texts.
B She plays in a rock band at school.
C They're over there on my granddad's boat.
D This is my favourite website for jeans.
E He's listening to music with his headphones.
F He often makes dinner for his family at the weekends.
G She's staying at Clare's house today.
H It's got a great camera on it.

Revision Units 1 – 2

GRAMMAR

1 Complete these questions with *much* or *many*.

1 How _much_ time do you spend on your computer?
2 How _____ texts do you send every day?
3 How _____ music do you download every month?
4 How _____ DVDs do you have?
5 How _____ shopping do you do online?
6 How _____ computer games do you own?
7 How _____ people in your class have a laptop?
8 How _____ does this computer game cost?

2 Complete the conversation with the present simple or present continuous form of the verbs in brackets. Use contractions where possible.

Emilia Hi, Isaac. What (1) _are you doing_ (you/do)?

Isaac Hi, Emilia. I (2) _____ (paint) a picture of my mum.

Emilia Is it for school?

Isaac No, it's for the art club. I (3) _____ (go) every Wednesday.

Emilia Oh, right. (4) _____ (be) it good fun?

Isaac Yes, I (5) _____ (love) it. We (6) _____ (learn) to paint faces at the moment.

Emilia (7) _____ (you/draw) as well?

Isaac Yes, we (8) _____ (do) different kinds of art every week.

Emilia Great! Can I join?

3 Put the words in the correct order to make sentences.

1 always / I / from / download / this website / my music / .
I always download my music from this website.
2 after school / watch / We / usually / DVDs / don't / .
3 with / sometimes / Oliver / photos / his mobile / takes / .
4 never / computer games / They / at school / play / .
5 chat / Sophie and Alex / don't / online / often / .
6 in the evenings / usually / on his laptop / works / My dad / .

4 Complete the advert with these words.

are   have   is   ~~looking~~   make   starting

Sanders Street Leisure Centre

New Computer Club!

Are you 1) _looking_ for a new hobby and 2) _____ you between 13 and 16 years old? Then we have the answer for you!

The leisure centre is 3) _____ a new computer club. It's on Thursday afternoons from 4 to 5.30 p.m.

At the club you can play computer games and also 4) _____ your own games. We 5) _____ more information online on our website. The club 6) _____ free but there are only 20 places.

We hope to see you soon!

03 We ♥ school

READING

1 Read the article and match these headings with the paragraphs.

> A special visitor   What the students think
> ~~Why is the Rosendale School library unusual?~~
> Team work!   Where the idea came from

1) _Why is the Rosendale School library unusual?_
For most students, their library is a room in the school with desks, chairs and lots of books. This is not true for the students of Rosendale School. Their library is an old red London bus!

2) _____
Rosendale School had lots of new students and not enough classrooms. They decided to change the library into a classroom. This gave the school another problem. They had no library. Then a parent had the great idea to use an old bus for the school library.

3) _____
It took eight months to change the bus into a library. Many people helped make the project possible. For example, students from the school helped paint the bus. Local businesses gave the school money and lots of local people worked free of charge. Everyone enjoyed working on the new library.

4) _____
When the library was ready, Rosendale School invited Michael Morpurgo to open it. Michael is a famous writer. He is the author of over 100 books, such as *The Butterfly Lion* and *War Horse*, which is now a film. Everyone at Rosendale School was very excited when he visited their library.

5) _____
Everyone loves it! The bus is a fantastic place to read and the students enjoy spending time there. The bus library was lots of fun to make and it is great fun to use.

2 Read the article and choose true (T) or false (F) for each sentence.

1 Rosendale School bought a new bus for their library. _F_
2 The old library is now used as a classroom. ___
3 A student had the idea for the library bus. ___
4 Local businesses helped pay for the library bus. ___
5 Michael Morpurgo is a teacher at Rosendale School. ___
6 Some of the students don't like the library bus. ___

VOCABULARY
School and education

1 Find and write eight school subjects.

k	g	e	c	u	g	e	l	i	h	b	m	d	s	s
i	h	t	s	m	b	t	k	f	s	o	t	m	e	r
m	e	s	r	u	n	y	o	i	n	c	e	i	l	i
l	n	h	i	s	t	o	r	y	e	k	d	o	n	e
o	i	o	p	i	n	c	e	n	t	u	i	n	o	d
p	m	u	o	c	i	s	o	b	t	s	o	p	s	y
o	a	c	n	u	k	i	w	s	o	c	u	n	m	p
l	(a	r	t)	j	i	c	r	o	c	i	k	n	a	d
l	s	b	u	a	s	e	n	t	o	e	n	u	t	r
i	w	a	x	b	t	u	o	n	i	n	n	c	h	e
t	o	n	i	u	c	o	m	p	u	c	a	t	s	o
i	n	o	p	e	d	i	a	s	n	e	a	p	s	d
g	o	m	a	t	s	y	u	d	i	o	m	u	i	o
i	o	n	w	g	e	o	g	r	a	p	h	y	s	a
c	r	a	n	k	i	o	n	i	c	a	w	h	o	c

1 _art_   5 _____
2 _____   6 _____
3 _____   7 _____
4 _____   8 _____

2 Match these places with the objects.

> ~~canteen~~   classroom   gym   library
> science lab   sports field

1 ____canteen____   2 _____

3 _____   4 _____

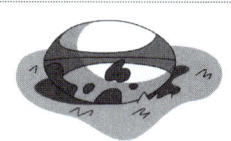

5 _____   6 _____

3 Complete the dialogues with these words.

> canteen   classroom   ~~gym~~   library
> science lab   sports field

1 Why have you got your sports bag, Alex?
  I've got basketball practice in the ____gym____ after school.
2 Are you having lunch in the _____, Lucy?
  No, I'm going home for lunch today.
3 Where are we having geography today?
  In _____ 12B. It's next to the gym.
4 Where are you going, Isobel?
  To the _____ . I've got chemistry now.
5 Where are you going with those maths books?
  I'm taking them back to the _____ .
6 What's happening on the _____ ?
  They're playing a football match.

4 Complete the table with these words and phrases.

> ~~an exam~~   a good mark   a language
> a prize   a school uniform   a test   a tie
> French   in your notebook   on the board

get	
have/do	an exam
learn	
wear	
write	

5 Choose the correct words.

1 I *had/wrote* a lot of history homework last night.
2 Most students in my country *do/wear* a uniform to school.
3 Emily *did/got* a good mark in her chemistry test.
4 The teacher *wrote/wore* the answers on the board.
5 I *wear/get* a red tie to school every day.
6 Every July we *write/have* exams.

6 Match the words (1–8) with the definitions (A–H).

1 board *E*
2 desk ____
3 exam ____
4 mark ____
5 notebook ____
6 pencil case ____
7 timetable ____
8 school uniform ____

A a list of times when classes start and finish
B a number or letter that shows how good a piece of work is
C a small bag where you keep your pens and pencils
D a special set of clothes that students wear for school
E something on the wall of a classroom that the teacher writes on
F a test of how much you know about something
G a book you can write in
H a table that you sit at to write or work

7 Choose the correct words.
1 The <u>music</u>/art teacher wasn't at school so we didn't have guitar practice today.
2 Your *timetable/board* shows you when lessons start and finish.
3 Henry got a good mark for his English language *prize/test*.
4 I can't go to the cinema. I've got a lot of *homework/exam* to do.
5 My school *tie/uniform* is a green sweater and a black skirt.
6 Jaya sits at the *desk/classroom* behind James.

8 Complete the text with the best answer, A, B or C, for each space.

MY SCHOOL

I like going to school because I see my best friends there. All the students wear a 1) <u>uniform</u> at my school. It's blue and it looks OK, but I don't like wearing a 2) _____ . It's so uncomfortable round my neck!

We don't sit in the same 3) _____ all day. We move for each lesson. I never remember what lesson I have so I'm always looking at my 4) _____ !

My favourite 5) _____ is French. Our French teacher is really cool. We never sit at our desks all lesson. We often get up and write on the 6) _____ . We had a French exam last week. I was really happy with my 7) _____ because I got 19/20.

I don't like history very much. Our history teacher always gives us lots of 8) _____ !

1 **A** uniform B bag C glasses
2 **A** skirt B trousers C tie
3 **A** table B classroom C teacher
4 **A** watch B pencil case C timetable
5 **A** subject B classroom C desk
6 **A** board B desk C pen
7 **A** classroom B timetable C mark
8 **A** games B homework C prizes

GRAMMAR
Past simple

1 Complete the table with the correct form of the verbs.

Infinitive	Past simple
write	1) *wrote*
2) _____	went
take	3) _____
4) _____	saw
choose	5) _____
6) _____	was/were
speak	7) _____
8) _____	began

2 Complete the sentences with was/were or wasn't/weren't.
1 It <u>was</u> Jonathan's first day at school today. He really enjoyed it.
2 I usually enjoy my lunch in the canteen, but today the food _____ very nice.
3 I don't usually like maths, but my lesson _____ really good today.
4 Jacob and Emily _____ at school today. They aren't very well.
5 My English homework _____ very difficult today. I finished it quickly.
6 I got a really good mark in my history exam. My parents _____ really happy.

3 Complete the short answers.
1 Were George and Harry in class today?
Yes, <u>they were</u> .
2 Was your homework difficult?
No, _____ .
3 Were your friends in the canteen at lunchtime?
Yes, _____ .
4 Was your school uniform red and grey?
Yes, _____ .
5 Were you nervous before your exam today, Joe?
No, _____ .
6 Was Anna the winner of the art prize this year?
Yes, _____ .

03 We ♥ school

4 Complete the sentences with the past simple form of the verbs in brackets.

1 Our teacher _wrote_ (write) the questions on the board.
2 I _____ (choose) Italian for my foreign language subject.
3 Mr Carter _____ (not give) us any geography homework yesterday.
4 Lee _____ (speak) to the PE teacher about the basketball match.
5 I _____ (have) lunch with Grace in the canteen.
6 The students _____ (not wear) school uniform yesterday.
7 We _____ (begin) the exam at 9.45 a.m.
8 My brother _____ (not go) to football practice today.

5 Complete the text with the correct form of the verbs in brackets.

My year in Greece

When I was 13 we 1) _lived_ (live) in Greece for a year. My school in Greece was called 'Gymnasio'. My school day 2) _____ (not be) the same as in the UK. In my Greek school, lessons 3) _____ (begin) at 8.15 and 4) _____ (finish) at 1.45.

The school 5) _____ (not have) a canteen. Everyone 6) _____ (go) home for lunch. We usually 7) _____ (have) lunch at about 2.30.

I loved the school summer holidays in Greece. They 8) _____ (be) three months long!

LISTENING

1 🔊 3.1 Listen to Nicola telling Tom about her homework and choose the correct answer, A or B.

1 Nicola watched a film. Which country was it about?
  (A) Bangladesh
  B Barbados
2 What kind of schools was the film about?
  A sailing schools
  B schools on boats
3 When do the students use the boat schools?
  A in the rainy season
  B all of the year
4 How do the computers on the boats work?
  A with solar power
  B with electricity
5 How do students get to the boat school?
  A They swim to the boat.
  B The boat picks them up.

2 🔊 3.2 Listen again and complete the sentences from Tom and Nicola's conversation.

1 Nicola watched a film about boat schools in her _geography_ lesson.
2 Each boat has a classroom with a _____ and desks.
3 Each boat has a classroom for about _____ students.
4 The boat is also like the school _____ . It picks students up from their houses.
5 Each boat library has about _____ books, as well as computers.

21

GRAMMAR
Past simple questions

1 Put the words in the correct order to make questions.

1 today / your maths exam / Was / difficult / ?
   Was your maths exam difficult today?
2 finish / you / your history homework / Did / ?
3 a good mark / Did / get / in his biology test / David / ?
4 the answer on the board / the teacher / Did / write / ?
5 your library books / Were / in your school bag / ?
6 Clare and Mark / lunch in the school canteen / Did / have / ?

2 Match the questions (1–6) with the answers (A–F).

1 Did Madeleine have a good English lesson? _B_
2 How much was it? ___
3 Did you get a good mark for your exam? ___
4 Where was your PE lesson today? ___
5 Did Jake and Sonia have school dinner today? ___
6 When did you leave school yesterday? ___

A At 3.15 p.m.
B Yes, she did.
C No, they didn't.
D £2.99.
E Yes, I did.
F In the gym.

3 Complete the email with these words.

did   didn't   had   saw   took   ~~was~~
was   went

Hi, Billy

How 1) _was_ your school trip?
2) _____ you have a good time? I came back from my school history trip yesterday.
We 3) _____ to London. We 4) _____ a really good time. We visited lots of old places. My favourite place 5) _____ the Tower of London. We also went to Buckingham Palace, but we 6) _____ see the Queen! I 7) _____ lots of photos for my school project. We also went to the cinema in Leicester Square one evening. We 8) _____ a really good film.

Speak soon,

Helen

SPEAKING SKILLS

1 Choose the correct answer.

1 What *did/do/does* you do last weekend?
2 Where did you *have/had/having* lunch?
3 *What/Who/Where* did you speak to?
4 *What/When/Did* Robert finish his homework yesterday?
5 *Were/Did/Was* your parents happy with your school marks?
6 Who *did/was/were* your best friend at primary school?

03 We ♥ school

2 Choose the correct answer, A, B or C.

1 Did you have maths this morning?
   A Yes, I had.
   (B) Yes, we did.
   C Yes, you did.
2 Did Lara have lunch in the school canteen today?
   A Yes, she did.
   B Yes, she does.
   C Yes, she have.
3 Was Emma at school yesterday?
   A No, she didn't.
   B No, she wasn't.
   C No, she weren't.
4 Were the books in the library?
   A Yes, they were.
   B Yes, they did.
   C Yes, they was.
5 Did everyone do the science exam?
   A Yes, they do.
   B Yes, they did.
   C Yes, they done.
6 Did John and Helen's teacher go on the school trip?
   A No, they didn't.
   B No, he wasn't.
   C No, she didn't.

WRITING

1 Read about Mark's first day at school. Put the things he did in the correct order.

had science	____	had history	____
had a break	____	had English	1
had maths	____	went to the canteen	____

Monday
Today was my first day at my new school. When Mum dropped me at the school gate, I was quite nervous, but the day went really well. My first lesson was English. It was OK, but a bit boring. Then we went to another classroom for maths. Our maths teacher was nice and I really enjoyed the lesson. After maths, we had a break and I met some other new students. They're called Matt and Joe and they're really cool – they're Manchester United fans, too! After that I had two hours of science. The science lab is amazing and we did a cool experiment. At lunchtime I met Matt and Joe again and we ate together in the canteen. I had history after lunch. The teacher was nice, but I was really tired and nearly fell asleep! I really like my new school.

2 Read about Kirsty's school trip. Complete the text with these words and phrases.

> Then   After Big Ben   After lunch   ~~First~~
> Before we left   At lunchtime

Friday
We went on a school trip to London today. It was great fun! 1 _First_ , we visited the Houses of Parliament. 2 _____ we saw Big Ben. Kate took a cool photo of me and Tom there.
3 _____ we went for a short walk by the river. I wanted to go on a boat trip, but we didn't have time. 4 _____ we went to Hyde Park and had a picnic. 5 _____ we went to the Science Museum. I thought museums are all boring, but it was really good. 6 _____ , we went to the museum gift shop. I bought a cool bag. I really want to go to London again soon!

3 Write a paragraph about a great day out you had with your friends or family. Write about where you went, who you went with and what you did. Remember to use ordering words and phrases.

04 What a bargain!

READING

1 Read the article and match the people (1–4) with the pictures (A–D).

A   B   C   D

Are you a happy shopper?

1 Nicole _B_
"Am I a happy shopper? No way! I think shopping is boring. I usually buy my school books and things on the Internet. It's easier than shopping in town. I choose them and my mum pays for them with her card. The prices are usually good. That always makes Mum happy!"

2 David ___
"Mmm ... I'm not sure. I like going to music shops. They're more interesting than clothes shops. I like to buy posters of my favourite bands for my bedroom. Last week I went to my favourite music shop with my cousin. He bought me a DVD of my favourite pop group in concert for my birthday."

3 Ellie ___
"Yes, I'm always a happy shopper, especially when I'm with my grandma. She lives in the city and every Sunday I go to a market with her. We always find bargains. Markets are better than shops. You pay with cash, but the prices are often lower than in the shops. I love earrings and hats, and I usually spend all my pocket money!"

4 Adam ___
"Yes, I am! I always go shopping with my friends. There's a big department store in the city and we go every Saturday. The clothes are cheaper than in the small shops in my town. We always try on jeans and T-shirts. I don't often buy things because I'm saving for a new MP3 player at the moment."

2 Find words in the article that match these meanings.

1 not spending: _saving_
2 not interesting: _____
3 how much something costs: _____
4 a big picture: _____
5 something for sale at a very good price: _____
6 something you wear on your head: _____

3 Complete the sentences with words from the article.

1 Adam goes shopping in a _department store_ in the city every Saturday.
2 Adam and his friends always _____ clothes.
3 Nicole buys _____ on the Internet.
4 Nicole's mum pays with a _____.
5 Ellie and her grandma go shopping at a _____.
6 Ellie buys things with her _____ money.

VOCABULARY
Shopping

1 Put the letters in the right order to make different types of shops.

1 lhcoste ohps — _clothes shop_
2 kuspemaretr — _____
3 ucsim hosp — _____
4 osokhobp — _____
5 tsorps hops — _____
6 pocmrute hsop — _____
7 armtke — _____
8 mtendparet rotes — _____

2 Match the meanings (1–6) with the words (A–F).

1 the opposite of *open* _C_
2 a person who buys something from a shop ___
3 someone who sells things in a shop ___
4 a large shop that sells many types of things ___
5 to put on clothes in a shop before you buy them ___
6 something that is less than its usual price ___

A customer
B shop assistant
C closed
D bargain
E try on
F department store

04 What a bargain!

3 Choose the correct words.
1 What's the *price*/*receipt* of this bag?
2 We have a great *card*/*market* in our town. It sells everything and is really cheap.
3 My mum bought the concert tickets online with her *card*/*cash*.
4 Have you got the *price*/*receipt* for my slippers, Mum? I want to return them to the shop.
5 Have you got any *cash*/*receipt*? They don't take cards in this shop.

4 Match these words with the pictures.

~~card~~   cash   market   price   receipt

1 ......card......

2 ....

3 ....

4 ....

5 ....

5 Complete the conversation with these words.

bargain   closed   customer   ~~department store~~   open   shop assistant   try on

Lara Hi, Emma. Did you know there's a new 1) *department store* in town?

Emma Yeah, I know, Hartley's. My cousin's a 2) .... there.

Lara Really? I went there at the weekend with my mum. I saw some great clothes. I want to 3) .... some jeans I saw.

Emma OK, great. My cousin said there are some half-price trainers, they're a real 4) ....! I want to get some with my birthday money. When do you want to go?

Lara Well, it's 5) .... every day. It's only 6) .... on Sunday afternoons.

Emma Great. Let's go tomorrow, then. And I think for the first month every new 7) .... gets a free magazine.

Lara Cool!

Emma Great! See you there at 11.

6 Match the sentence beginnings (1–6) with the endings (a–f).

1 I'm saving
2 My dad paid
3 It cost
4 I bought
5 Thomas sold
6 We spent

a us nothing. It was free.
b a new dress for my party.
c his bike to a friend.
d the bill in the restaurant.
e money for a holiday.
f a lot of money on computer games.

7 Choose the correct words.

1 My new jeans were a bargain. They only *paid/cost* £15.
2 Fiona's *saving/collecting* her birthday money because she wants to buy a guitar.
3 They *bought/paid* a new computer game at the weekend.
4 Noah doesn't *buy/spend* a lot of money on music.
5 My grandma *paid/bought* for my tennis lessons.
6 How much does this bracelet *buy/cost*?

8 Match the questions (1–7) with the answers (A–G).

1 How much are these jeans? *D*
2 Where are the customer toilets? ___
3 Have you got your receipt? ___
4 Can I pay by card? ___
5 How much is this book? ___
6 Where's the shop assistant? ___
7 Excuse me. Can I try on this jacket? ___

A Next to the men's clothing department.
B Sorry, we only take cash.
C The price is on the back of it.
D They're £59.99.
E Over there. She's wearing a red uniform.
F Yes, of course. There's a mirror over there, near the entrance.
G Yes, it's in my bag.

GRAMMAR
Comparative adjectives

1 Complete the table with the comparative form of these adjectives.

bad big busy difficult expensive
good pretty short

-er	-ier	more + adjective	irregular
			worse

2 Choose the correct words.

1 The jacket is *more expensive*/*expensiver* than the trousers.
2 The green bag is *nicer/more nice* than the red one.
3 The shop assistants are *helpfuller/more helpful* here than in the other shop.
4 Online shopping is *more easy/easier* than going to the shops.
5 The sports clothes in the market are *cheaper/more cheaper* than the ones here.
6 The prices are *better/more good* here than in the other shop.

3 Complete the sentences with the comparative form of the adjectives in brackets.

1 Your jacket is *newer* (new) than mine.
2 This book is _____ (interesting) than that one.
3 I think shopping is _____ (boring) than doing homework.
4 Their shopping bags are _____ (heavy) than ours.
5 This birthday card is _____ (funny) than the other one.
6 The music in this shop is _____ (bad) than in the last shop.
7 I think the red dress is _____ (beautiful) than the blue one.
8 This music shop is _____ (big) than the one in my town.

04 What a bargain!

LISTENING

1 🔊 **4.1 Listen to five conversations. Choose the correct answer, A, B or C.**

1 What does Tom want to buy? _B_

 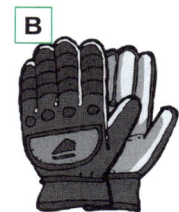 

2 Who gave Suzie her watch? ____

3 What did David buy online? ____

4 What time does the sports shop close on Sundays? ____

5 How much were Tim's jeans? ____

2 🔊 **4.2 Listen again and choose the correct answers.**

1 It is Tom's *brother's*/*cousin's* birthday.
2 Suzie's going *to her grandma's house*/*shopping*.
3 The girl wants to go to the *supermarket*/*bookshop*.
4 The girl wants to buy a *bag*/*ball* from the sports shop.
5 Tim bought his jeans from the website *Clotheswise*/*Clothessite*.

GRAMMAR
Superlative adjectives

1 Complete the table.

Adjective	Superlative
popular	1) _most popular_
2) _____	worst
big	3) _____
4) _____	farthest/furthest
difficult	5) _____
6) _____	lightest
good	7) _____
8) _____	friendliest
lonely	9) _____
10) _____	cheapest
funny	11) _____
12) _____	laziest
exciting	13) _____
14) _____	busiest
boring	15) _____

2 Complete the sentences with the superlative form of these words.

> ~~expensive~~   heavy   old   small
> tasty   young

1 This is the _most expensive_ phone in the shop.

2 This is Joshua's _____ pair of jeans.

3 My rucksack is the _____ .

4 Sally is the _____ shop assistant.

5 I like the _____ bag.

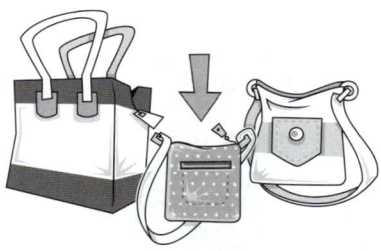

6 This is the _____ cake.

3 Choose the correct words.

1 The clothes are *cheaper*/*cheapest* here than in the last shop.
2 I've got the *most heaviest*/*heaviest* shopping bags.
3 Frank is *younger*/*youngest* than Lilly.
4 Our bill was *bigger*/*biggest* than yours.
5 The market was *busiest*/*busier* than the supermarket.
6 There are lots of clothes shops in my town, but Hardy's is the *most*/*more* popular.

4 Complete the sentences with one word in each space.

1 This is _the_ best sports shop in town.
2 Shopping online is often cheaper _____ buying things at the shops.
3 Your trainers are _____ expensive than mine.
4 The department store is busier at the weekend _____ in the week.
5 It's always _____ fun shopping with friends than with your parents.
6 This is _____ worst clothes shop in my town.

04 What a bargain!

5 Complete the review with the best answer, A, B or C for each space.

Some people say New York is a great city for shopping. What do I think? – Yes! I went shopping in New York last weekend and had the 1) *most amazing* shopping experience. Why? There are lots of reasons. Firstly, the shops are 2) _____ than the shops in my city and there is so much choice. Secondly, the shop assistants are 3) _____ than in many other places. You can also find 4) _____ bargains in New York! I bought some jeans and they were $30 5) _____ than the normal price. There are also lots of 6) _____ places to stop and have lunch. My favourite is Papa Joe's Pizzeria. They make the 7) _____ pizzas!

1 A amazing (B) most amazing C more amazing
2 A big B biggest C bigger
3 A friendlier B friendliest C friendly
4 A greatest B great C greater than
5 A cheap B cheapest C cheaper
6 A cool B cooler C coolest
7 A good B better C best

SPEAKING SKILLS

1 Complete the conversation with these phrases.

Thanks. I love it!   Can I try it on?
It's really nice. How much is it?   Yes, please.
~~Hi. Can I have a look at that red hat, please?~~
Oh. Have you got anything cheaper?

Man: Hello, can I help you?
Girl: 1) *Hi. Can I have a look at that red hat, please?*
Man: Yes, sure. Here you are.
Girl: 2) _____
Man: Let's have a look. It's £12.
Girl: 3) _____
Man: Yes, this one's only £6.99.
Girl: 4) _____
Man: Yes, of course. Here's a mirror.
Girl: 5) _____
Man: Shall I put it in a bag for you?
Girl: 6) _____

2 Choose the correct answer, A, B or C.

1 Can I try this T-shirt on, please?
  A Yes, you can try.   (B) Yes, of course.
  C Yes, you do.
2 Can I look at those earrings, please?
  A Yes, you look here.   B Yes, here you are.
  C Yes, those are.
3 Have you got anything bigger?
  A Yes, these are size 42.
  B Yes, these are smaller.
  C Yes, these are £14.
4 Have you got any other computer games?
  A Sorry, we aren't.
  B Sorry, we don't have any cheaper ones.
  C Sorry, that's all we've got.
5 Do you want your receipt in your bag?
  A Yes, I have a receipt.   B Yes, it's in my bag.
  C Yes, please.

WRITING

1 Match the sentences (A–H) with the headings (1–4) to describe people's favourite shops.

1 Where it is: *B*
2 Name of shop: _____
3 What it sells: _____
4 The best thing about it: _____

A My favourite shop's called Tara.
B It's in Sydney.
C I love the prices – you can find real bargains.
D It sells DVDs, CDs and T-shirts.
E Match Point is my favourite shop.
F The best thing is that it's near my school.
G You can buy paper and pens in this shop.
H It's in Madrid.

2 Complete Rosie's description of her favourite shop with one word for each space.

Hi. My name 1) *is* Rosie. My favourite shop's called Rainbow. It's 2) _____ Toronto. Rainbow sells clothes 3) _____ shoes. 4) _____ best thing about this shop is the jeans they sell. 5) _____ love going there with my friends. The worst 6) _____ about the shop is that it's always busy.

3 Write about your favourite place in your town (café, sports centre, etc.). Include where it is, how often you go there and why you like it.

Revision Units 3 – 4

VOCABULARY

1 Match these words with the correct meaning.

> canteen ~~cash~~ classroom gym library
> market price receipt

1 This is money in coins or notes.
   cash
2 This is a place you do exercise.
   ....
3 You get this piece of paper when you buy something.
   ....
4 This is where you eat lunch at school.
   ....
5 This is how much something costs.
   ....
6 There are lots of books in this place.
   ....
7 There are desks and a board in this place.
   ....
8 People buy and sell things in this place.
   ....

2 Choose the correct verbs.

1 Hannah *did/got* a prize for her painting.
2 Mark and Andrew *have/wear* a blue uniform to school.
3 We *had/wrote* a geography exam last Monday.
4 My parents *paid/bought* my new bike for me.
5 We didn't *learn/have* French lessons at primary school.
6 Tom *spent/saved* all his birthday money on a new guitar.

3 Choose the correct words.

1 Why didn't you buy the skirt you liked?
   Because the shop was *closed/open* when I arrived.
2 Do you like these jeans? I bought them yesterday.
   Yes, they're great. How much did they *pay/cost*?
3 I bought this jacket yesterday, but it's the wrong size. Can I change it?
   Yes, of course. Have you got your *receipt/bargain*?
4 Excuse me, have you got a smaller jacket?
   Yes, here you are. Would you like to *try/have* it on?
5 I like this bag. How much is it?
   Oh, it's a real *price/bargain*. It's only £12.
6 Who *paid/spent* for your football lessons?
   I did. I saved all my birthday money.

4 Complete Charlotte's diary with these words.

> assistant case field homework
> lesson shopping ~~teacher~~ test

Tuesday 8 June
Today didn't start very well! I got to school late and my 1) _teacher_ wasn't very happy with me. My first 2) .... was maths. We had a 3) .... – it was really difficult! French was OK, but Mrs Chevalier gave us lots of 4) .... to do! In the afternoon I had PE and we played hockey on the sports 5) .... It was a great game and our team won. After school I went 6) .... with Mum. She bought me a new pencil 7) .... and some cool trainers. The shop 8) .... gave me a free drinks bottle with my trainers. Then Mum took me for a burger and chips. We saw the new boy from school with his dad.

Revision Units 3 – 4

GRAMMAR

1 **Complete these sentences with the comparative or superlative form of the adjectives in brackets.**

1 Riverside is _the largest_ (large) secondary school in the city.
2 Yasmin got a _____ (high) mark in her test than Annabel.
3 I think Mr Unwin is _____ (funny) teacher at school.
4 History is _____ (difficult) subject at school.
5 Your school uniform is _____ (bad) than mine.
6 Gareth got a prize for _____ (good) science project.
7 Sally's got _____ (neat) handwriting in the class.
8 Our new library is _____ (big) than our old one.

2 **Complete Amy's email with the past simple form of these verbs.**

> be   buy   ~~go~~   have   see   spend   stop
> take

Hi Harriet

How are you? I 1) _went_ shopping in London with my parents yesterday. There 2) _____ lots of fantastic clothes shops. I 3) _____ two new tops and a pair of jeans. We 4) _____ at a café in Covent Garden for lunch. I 5) _____ a really cool girl there. She 6) _____ purple hair and a white leather dress! In the afternoon we 7) _____ my little brother to Hamley's. It's the world's largest toyshop. We 8) _____ lots of money there!

See you at school tomorrow.

Love Amy x

3 **Complete the short answers.**

1 Did Mark buy an expensive jacket?
   Yes, _he did_ .
2 Were Jamie and Zoe in school today?
   No, _____ .
3 Was your homework easy?
   No, _____ .
4 Did you like your school lunch?
   Yes, _____ .
5 Was this your best mark for English?
   Yes, _____ .
6 Did your sister go on the school trip with you?
   No, _____ .

4 **Choose the best answer, A, B or C.**

1 The shoes are more expensive here _than_ in the other shop.
   A with   B from   **C than**
2 Freddie _____ his school tie in the gym yesterday.
   A leave   B left   C leaves
3 What mark did Annalise _____ in her English exam last week?
   A got   B get   C gets
4 Is this _____ cheapest bookshop in town?
   A the   B a   C one
5 Rachel is _____ than Tom at maths.
   A good   B better   C best
6 Ms Pinner _____ teach me science last year.
   A didn't   B doesn't   C don't

31

05 Mysteries from history

READING

1 Read the story and choose true (T) or false (F) for each sentence.

1 The dancing plague happened in the summer of 1518. _T_
2 Frau Troffea was visiting Strasbourg. ____
3 Frau Troffea looked very happy when she was dancing. ____
4 The people danced in the day and went home at night. ____
5 The dancing plague lasted from July to September. ____
6 Experts now know why the people were dancing. ____

The dancing plague of 1518

In July of 1518 something strange happened in the city of Strasbourg, France. A woman called Frau Troffea began to dance in front of her neighbours. This perhaps doesn't sound very strange, but she danced for about five days, without stopping! There was no music and her face showed no sign of happiness.

At first, people in the city believed the woman was mad. Then one of her neighbours joined her, and then another. After a week a lot of people were dancing in the streets of Strasbourg. They were dancing day and night without stopping. After a month there were about 400 people dancing.

Some of the dancers died because they were very tired. Strangely, some doctors believed the best medicine for the dancers was more dancing! The city authorities opened dance halls and paid musicians to play for the dancers. They even paid professional dancers to join them. Finally, in early September, the people slowly stopped dancing and went home.

Nobody understands what happened in Strasbourg, but there are two main ideas. One idea is that there was something wrong with their food. Other people think it was because of stress. At that time the people of Strasbourg had very hard and difficult lives. They were often sick and hungry. Some people believe that they just went a bit mad.

2 Read the story again and choose the correct answer, A, B or C.

1 What did Frau Troffea's neighbours think when she started dancing?
  A She was happy.
  B She was a professional dancer.
  C She was mad.
2 Who was the first person to dance with Frau Troffea?
  A a doctor   B a musician   C a neighbour
3 How many people were dancing by August?
  A 400   B 40   C 4,000
4 Why did some of the dancers die?
  A Because they didn't eat anything.
  B Because they were very tired.
  C Because they had difficult lives.
5 Who paid the musicians to play music?
  A the dancers
  B the Strasbourg authorities
  C Frau Troffea's neighbours
6 What kind of life did the people of Strasbourg have in 1518?
  A easy and fun   B poor but happy
  C hard and difficult

VOCABULARY
Dates and times

1 Match these words with the meanings.

> ancient   battle   castle   famous
> king   ~~queen~~   treasure

1 a female head of a country
   queen
2 a large strong building with high walls
   ____
3 from a long time ago
   ____
4 a male head of a country
   ____
5 something or someone that many people know
   ____
6 a fight between two armies in a war
   ____
7 valuable objects such as gold, silver and jewellery
   ____

05 Mysteries from history

2 Complete the sentences with these words.

> ancient   battle   Castle   famous   ~~king~~   treasure

1 Tutankhamun was a _king_ in Egypt.
2 The .... Greeks held the first Olympic Games.
3 Lots of people know about the Colosseum in Rome. It's very ....
4 The .... of Little Bighorn in 1876 was between the US army and the Native Americans.
5 The pirates found .... on the ship. It was a big box of gold jewellery.
6 No kings or queens live in Chapultepec .... in Mexico. It is a museum.

3 Complete the table with these words and phrases.

> ~~2.30 p.m.~~   25 May 1975   April 2008
> the twenty-first century   2 January 1952
> the beginning of last year   12 o'clock

at	_2.30 p.m._
in	
on	

4 Choose the best answer, A, B or C.

1 It's my brother's birthday __on__ Friday.
   Ⓐ on   B at   C in
2 The battle finished on ....
   A 26 June 1876   B June 1876   C 1876
3 The museum opened .... the end of last year.
   A in   B at   C on
4 Queen Isabella I of Castile was born .... 22 April 1451.
   A on   B at   C in
5 They found the treasure of Gourdon in France in the middle .... the nineteenth century.
   A to   B on   C of
6 A Queen lived in the castle many years ....
   A from   B ago   C for

5 Find and write six adjectives.

g	o	u	g	l	d	l	e	s	k
o	n	t	e	o	a	h	n	r	y
n	t	i	n	f	n	o	a	f	e
c	o	h	d	s	g	d	e	r	t
l	i	g	h	t	e	m	a	n	d
e	l	l	e	a	r	o	u	c	e
e	n	o	l	l	o	g	i	l	t
n	o	n	u	s	u	n	t	e	r
k	r	a	a	d	s	c	e	a	n
s	o	d	i	r	t	y	i	n	n

1 _loud_
2 ....
3 ....
4 ....
5 ....
6 ....

6 Choose the correct words.

1 It's not a good idea to walk here at night. It's very safe/_dangerous_.
2 This city is very dirty/clean. There's rubbish everywhere.
3 Before electricity, homes were often very light/dark.
4 Life was very hard for poor/rich people in Victorian England.
5 The sound of the battle was very loud/quiet. You could hear it for miles.
6 In history it was always rich/quiet people who lived in castles.

7 Choose the odd one out.

1. the 1980s
   1200 BC
   December
   the sixteenth century
2. castle
   treasure
   palace
   museum
3. battle
   famous
   quiet
   ancient
4. 12 o'clock
   2001
   in the morning
   4.55 p.m.
5. queen
   tower
   prince
   king
6. dangerous
   history
   poor
   dirty

8 Complete the text with these words.

1901   dangerous   dark   in   poor
queen   rich

What was life like in Victorian times?

The Victorian times started 1) *in* 1837 and ended in 2) _____ . This is when Victoria was 3) _____ of Britain. The people who lived in Britain at this time were called Victorians. Many 4) _____ Victorians had an easy and comfortable life, but 5) _____ Victorians had a very hard life. Many poor people lived in 6) _____ , dirty houses. Their jobs were sometimes 7) _____ and they worked long hours.

GRAMMAR
Past continuous

1 Choose the correct words.

1. The king *eat/was eating* dinner.
2. Mark and Jane *was/were* visiting a castle.
3. He *watch/was watching* a film about the Romans.
4. We *was/were* looking at a website about the pyramids.
5. Martin *search/was searching* for treasure.
6. I *was/were* listening to a radio programme about the Incas.

2 Make sentences. Use the past continuous.

1. the soldiers / fight / in the battle
   The soldiers were fighting in the battle.
2. the children / hide / the treasure / ?
   _____
3. the king and queen / not stay / in the castle
   _____
4. we / study / ancient Greece
   _____
5. Henry / not speak / to his brother
   _____
6. she / visit / the Natural History Museum / ?
   _____

3 Complete the short answers.

1. Were you visiting the museum when you saw Mark?
   Yes, *I was* .
2. Were they studying the Romans in their history lesson on Monday?
   Yes, _____ .
3. Was he searching for treasure when he found the cave?
   No, _____ .
4. Were you waiting for a long time, Alice?
   No, _____ .
5. Were the Aztecs in Mexico in the fourteenth to sixteenth centuries?
   Yes, _____ .
6. Were your parents watching a film when you got home?
   No, _____ .

05 Mysteries from history

4 Complete the sentences with the past simple or past continuous form of the verbs in brackets.

1. She *was watching* (watch) the news when she *heard* (hear) the loud noise outside.
2. Kieran and Joe _____ (find) the old watch when they _____ (dig) in the school garden.
3. I _____ (stand) outside the palace when I _____ (see) the queen.
4. We _____ (work) on the computer when the room suddenly _____ (go) dark.
5. The tour guide _____ (tell) us about the castle when my phone _____ (ring).
6. The man _____ (drive) home when the police _____ (stop) him.
7. They _____ (have) dinner when they _____ (hear) the news.
8. Laura _____ (watch) a film when she _____ (fall) asleep.

5 Complete the text with the best answer, A, B or C, for each space.

Treasure!

It was the end of the summer and my brother and I 1) *were* spending our last day at the beach. It was a hot day and the sun was shining so we 2)____ to go for a swim. We 3)____ in the sea when we noticed a dark hole in the rocks. We swam closer and realised it was a cave. We 4)____ feeling a bit scared, but decided to swim inside. When we got inside we 5)____ something bright at the back of the cave. It 6)____ shining and looked like silver. 'Treasure!' we both 7)____ . When we reached it, we both laughed. It 8)____ treasure, it was some old tin cans!

1. A was B) were C is
2. A decided B deciding C decide
3. A swim B swam C were swimming
4. A was B were C is
5. A seeing B see C saw
6. A is B was C were
7. A shouted B shouting C shout
8. A weren't B isn't C wasn't

LISTENING

1 🔊 5.1 Listen to Paul talking to Louise about a news story. What did the boy in the story find? Choose one answer.

1. some coins
2. a map
3. gold
4. a bottle
5. a necklace
6. a plate

2 🔊 5.2 Listen again and choose the correct answer, A, B or C.

1. What was Paul doing on the computer?
   A He was doing his homework.
   B) He was reading the news.
   C He was playing a computer game.
2. Where did the boy find the bottle?
   A in a house
   B in a garden
   C on the beach
3. Where did the bottle come from?
   A Canada
   B Ireland
   C England
4. Who wrote the message in the bottle?
   A two girls
   B two boys
   C a boy and a girl
5. How did the women learn that someone found their message?
   A A friend told them.
   B The boy wrote to them.
   C They heard it on the news.
6. How did the women and the boy speak to each other?
   A on the telephone
   B on Skype
   C face to face

GRAMMAR
Defining relative clauses

1 Put the words in the correct order to make sentences.

1 who / These are / lived in Windsor Castle / the kings / .
   These are the kings who lived in Windsor Castle.

2 who / Harry is / found the treasure / the boy / .

3 went to London / are / who / the students / Where / ?

4 about dinosaurs / a book / is / I'm reading / which / .

5 is / which / They've got / 300 years old / a painting / .

6 works / That's the man / in the museum / who / .

7 was on my desk / the map / Where's / that / ?

8 has information / that / This is the website / about Henry VIII / .

2 Choose the correct words.

1 A castle is a building *that/who* often has towers.
2 I met somebody *which/who* lives near the Acropolis in Athens.
3 Anna works in a shop *which/who* sells lots of old things.
4 The letter *that/who* is on the table is about my history trip.
5 We live in the house *that/who* my grandfather built.
6 We had a history test *that/who* was very difficult.

3 Complete the text with these words.

> making   standing   talking   that
> ~~was~~   was   who   who

One day last week I 1) *was* walking home from school. I was on the road 2) _____ goes past the old castle. I was 3) _____ on my mobile phone to my friend 4) _____ was telling me a joke. I 5) _____ laughing a lot when someone said to me 'Sshh! Can you be quiet, please?' When I turned around I saw a man in old clothes. He was 6) _____ at one of the open windows in the castle. He looked angry. I switched off my phone. When I looked at the castle again, the man wasn't there. Where was the man 7) _____ spoke to me? I knew the castle wasn't someone's home. I was a bit scared. The next day I heard in the news that a TV company was 8) _____ a film in the castle. The man who was wearing old clothes was an actor!

36 GOLD EXPERIENCE

Mysteries from history

SPEAKING SKILLS

1 Match the phrases (1–6) with the correct places (A–F) on the map.

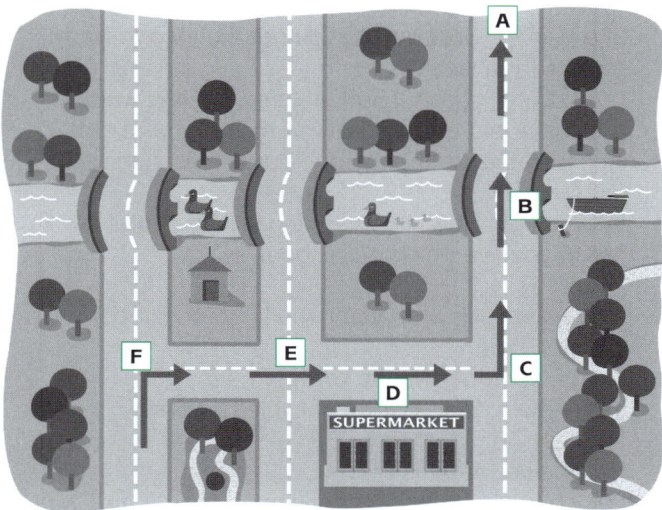

1 turn right   *F*
2 go over the bridge
3 go past the supermarket
4 turn left
5 cross the road
6 go straight on

2 Put the words in the correct order.

1 tell / you / me / Can / where / , / the / please / cinema / is? /
   Can you tell me where the cinema is, please?

2 right / church / . / and / go / Turn / past / the

3 tell / Can / shops / you / ? / me / where / , / the / are / please /

4 the / and / they're / Go / on / your / bridge / left / . / over

5 you / ? / tell / get / Can / me / to / to / Street / Brook / how

6 on / straight / and / second / it's / the / Go / road / on / your / . / right /

WRITING

1 Complete the sentences with the correct form of the verbs in brackets.

A) A few seconds later we 1) *heard* (hear) a vase smash on the floor. We 2) _____ (be) really scared. What 3) _____ (be) in the room with us?

B) Last Saturday I 4) _____ (be) at my cousin's house. We 5) _____ (watch) a scary film on TV when something strange happened.

C) Then, suddenly, the lights 6) _____ (come) back on. We 7) _____ (see) my cousin's cat run out of the living room. It 8) _____ (be) the cat that broke the vase!

D) In the middle of the film, all the lights and the TV suddenly 9) _____ (stop) working. It 10) _____ (be) very dark.

2 Put the paragraphs of the story in the correct order.

1   *B*
2
3
4

3 Write a short story. Start your story with these words:

A strange thing happened to me on the way to school yesterday.

06 Have a good trip!

READING

1 Read the introduction to an interview and choose the best title.

- A My family's favourite hobby
- B The fastest way to travel
- C A week on two wheels

1) _____
How does your family travel during the week? By car, by bus or by train? Next week one family in Manchester is trying something for the first time: they are going to do all their travelling by bike. I spoke to the children of the family, Lucy and Oliver Morris.

Interviewer: So, how did you get the idea to travel by bike for a week?
Lucy: 1) *Our school had the idea.* They want us to think about how we can be healthier and also kinder to the planet. My dad says it will also save us money!
Interviewer: How much cycling will you do? How far do you live from your school?
Oliver: 2) _____
Interviewer: How do you usually get to school?
Oliver: 3) _____ My mum drives us on her way to work.
Interviewer: Will your mum cycle to work?
Lucy: 4) _____
Interviewer: Why is that?
Lucy: I think the last time my mum rode a bike was about ten years ago!
Interviewer: How about your dad's journey to work?
Oliver: 5) _____ He catches a train and then catches a bus. He works in the city.
Interviewer: And is he going to cycle to work?
Lucy: 6) _____ He'll still take the train. He'll cycle to the station, take his bike on the train and then cycle to his office.
Interviewer: Well, good luck! I think it's a great idea and I hope you all enjoy it.
Lucy & Oliver: Thanks!

2 Read the interview. Choose which sentence fits each space. You do not need all the sentences.

> It's a good idea to travel by bike for a week.
> By car. No, it's too far.
> He usually drives to the train station.
> We usually get to school at 8.45 a.m.
> It will take us about fifteen minutes to cycle to school.
> ~~Our school had the idea~~.
> Yes, but she's going to find it difficult!

VOCABULARY
Travel and transport

1 Complete the table with these words.

> ~~bike~~ coach ferry helicopter motorbike
> plane ship train tram yacht

Land	Air	Sea
bike		

06 Have a good trip!

2 Choose the correct words.

1. Are you taking your *bike*/*motorbike* on holiday with you?
   Yes, we're going to go cycling in the mountains.
2. Do you walk to school?
   No, I take the school *bus*/*yacht*.
3. Is your brother on a school trip?
   Yes. He's in Switzerland. They're on a *coach*/*ferry* trip through the mountains.
4. How do you travel between the islands?
   There's a small *ship*/*ferry*. It carries about thirty passengers.
5. What did you do for your birthday?
   My uncle took me on a *helicopter*/*motorbike* ride. It was my first time flying.
6. How long does it take you to travel to Moscow?
   About five hours. We usually go by *tram*/*train*.
7. Cannes is a very popular place for the rich and famous.
   Yes, you can see some amazing *helicopters*/*yachts* in the harbour.
8. What's the best way to get to the central library?
   Take the *tram*/*coach* because the traffic is always bad in the city centre.

3 Complete the text with these words.

> catch   drive   ferry   go   helicopter
> journey   on foot   ~~trams~~

Hi. My name's Pedro and I live on an island. The island's not big and there are no buses or 1) _trams_ so I usually go everywhere 2) _____ . My parents both 3) _____ , but they sold their car when we moved to the island. Every month we 4) _____ to the city on the mainland. First we take the 5) _____ from the harbour, and then we 6) _____ the train to the city centre. I really enjoy the 7) _____ . There is a rich businessman who lives on my island. I know he has a 8) _____ and flies to the mainland. I think that's a really cool way to travel!

4 Match these places with the pictures.

> airport   ~~bus stop~~   coach station   harbour
> port   train station

1 _bus stop_

2 _____

3 _____

4 _____

5 _____

6 _____

5 Match the words in bold with the meanings.

1. Can all **passengers** travelling to Gloucester please get off the train now? _B_
2. How much is a train **ticket** to Istanbul? ___
3. The school is organising a weekend **trip** to Madrid. ___
4. The bus **driver** will tell you which bus stop you need. ___
5. We apologise for the **delay** to the 10.45 train to London. This train will now leave at 11.30. ___
6. Please do not leave any **luggage** in front of the train doors. ___

A someone who drives a vehicle
B people who use a kind of transport but are not driving it, flying it or sailing it
C when you go somewhere, usually for a short time, and come back again
D when something happens later than you planned or expected
E the bags and suitcases that you take with you when you are travelling
F a small piece of paper or card to show you paid for a journey

6 Choose the correct words.

1 How much *tickets*/*luggage* are you taking? I've only got one suitcase.
2 We are coming back from our skiing *trip*/*delay* late on Sunday evening.
3 The train didn't leave on time because the *driver*/*passenger* was having a tea break.
4 You need to buy a *harbour*/*ticket* before you get on the ferry.
5 I'll meet you at the *bus stop*/*bus station* near my house. It's the one in front of the post box.
6 These seats are for *tickets*/*passengers* who are old or disabled.

7 Complete the sentences with these words.

> drives   drove   fly   ~~ride~~   rides   sailed

1 I learned to ___ride___ a horse when I was six.
2 The fisherman _____ out to sea in his fishing boat.
3 My uncle worked in London last year. He _____ a black taxi.
4 One day I'd like to learn to _____ a helicopter.
5 My brother is 18 and he _____ a motorbike.
6 My mum's a bus driver. She _____ the school bus.

8 Choose the correct words.

Hi, Jane
I'm so excited! We're going to visit my cousins in Australia next week. We're going to 1) *drive*/*take* a coach to Heathrow Airport. Then we're 2) *catching*/*flying* a plane to Singapore. We'll stay there for a few days and then 3) *ride*/*take* another plane to Australia. We're arriving in Sydney late at night. My uncle's meeting us at the 4) *airport*/*station* and he'll 5) *catch*/*drive* us to his house in Newcastle. My uncle's got a boat and he says he'll teach me to 6) *ride*/*sail*! I'll call you when I'm back.
Adam

GRAMMAR
going to

1 Make questions. Use *going to*.

1 you / travel / to Morocco / by plane / ?
   ___Are you going to travel to Morocco by plane?___
2 we / stay / for seven nights / ?
   _____
3 she / stay / with a family in Brazil / ?
   _____
4 what / you / do / next summer / ?
   _____
5 when / she / learn to drive / ?
   _____
6 Jacob / cycle / to school tomorrow / ?
   _____
7 they / meet / at the coach station / ?
   _____

2 Match the answers with the questions in Exercise 1.

a I'm going to stay with my grandparents. _4_
b No, she isn't. ___
c No, they're going to meet at the train station. ___
d When she's twenty. ___
e Yes, he is. ___
f Yes, I am. ___
g Yes, we are. ___

06 Have a good trip!

3 Complete Harriet's plans for the weekend. Use *going to* and the verbs in brackets.

My friend Francesca 1) *'s going to spend* (spend) this weekend with me. I 2) _____ (meet) her on Saturday morning at the train station and we 3) _____ (walk) to the shopping centre. She wants to buy a new coat, but I 4) _____ (not buy) anything. In the evening we 5) _____ (see) some other friends and watch a DVD together. Francesca 6) _____ (stay) the night at my house. On Sunday we 7) _____ (not do) anything – just relax!

will

4 Complete the sentences with these verbs. Use *will* or *won't*.

be   buy   ~~catch~~   leave   take   walk

1 Tom's mum usually drives him home from school, but today he *will catch* the bus.
2 We _____ to the party because it's raining.
3 Next year my uncle _____ us to the South of France. He's very rich and has a yacht.
4 Kirsty _____ late for dinner because she missed her bus.
5 Liam's parents _____ him a motorbike. They think motorbikes are dangerous.
6 The ferry _____ on time because of the bad weather.

5 Complete the questions with *will* and these verbs. Complete the short answers with *will* or *won't*.

buy   have   miss   ~~phone~~   send   take

1 *Will* you *phone* me tomorrow evening from your hotel room?
Yes, I *will* .
2 _____ she _____ a lot of luggage with her when she comes?
No, she _____ .
3 _____ they _____ their friends and family?
Yes, they _____ .
4 _____ we _____ our tickets before we go?
No, we _____ .
5 _____ he _____ lots of photos to show us?
Yes, he _____ .
6 _____ you _____ me an email?
Yes, I _____ .

LISTENING

1 🔊 **6.1** Listen to a teacher talking about plans for a school trip. Choose the words you hear.
1 bus
2 <u>train</u>
3 ship
4 bicycle
5 ticket
6 coach
7 port

2 🔊 **6.2** Listen again and complete the notes.

School trip
1 Place: *Port* Greenway
2 Day: _____
3 Meet at: the _____
4 Leave at: _____ a.m.
5 Wear: _____ clothes
6 Cost: £ _____

GRAMMAR
Present continuous for future

1 Complete the sentences. Use the present continuous form of the verbs in brackets.

1 Here are your tickets. The ferry *'s leaving* (leave) in ten minutes.
2 Rachel _____ (not come) on the trip tomorrow. She's not very well.
3 Here's a picture of our new car. Mum _____ (collect) it from the garage next week.
4 I can't come with you to the café. I _____ (meet) my cousins at the train station in five minutes.
5 My brother _____ (go) to a motorbike show on Saturday. He got tickets for his birthday.
6 Simon _____ (not see) Will and Suzie this evening. He's got too much homework to do.
7 My Dad's got to go to Italy for work. He _____ (fly) from London airport this afternoon.
8 Lisa and Ellie _____ (not watch) the film this afternoon. They saw it last week.

2 Complete the information sheet with one word in each space.

Class 9B school trip to Paris

This year our class 1) *is* going to visit Paris for our school trip. We 2) _____ going to stay in Paris for two nights. We're travelling 3) _____ the port of Dover 4) _____ coach and catching a ferry to France. Then we 5) _____ travelling by coach to Paris. We're 6) _____ to stay in a hotel in the centre of the city. The trip 7) _____ cost £159 per student.

06 Have a good trip!

SPEAKING SKILLS

1 Put the words in the correct order.

1 are / going to / ? / see / in the holidays / Who / you
   Who are you going to see in the holidays?

2 you / What / going to / ? / are / do

3 in Santiago / it / ? / be / Will / hot

4 ? / you / going / to the beach / Are / next week /

5 is / it / ? / going to / What / cost

6 you / are / When / going / ? / to Turkey

2 Read the conversation and choose the correct words.

Michael: What are you 1) *going to/will* do in the summer, Kerry?
Kerry: I'm going to Switzerland. How 2) *about/for* you?
Michael: I'm staying here. I'm going to go to a football camp with my sister. Where 3) *are/will* you going to stay in Switzerland?
Kerry: With my grandparents in Bern. They live there.
Michael: Great! 4) *Will/Is* it be hot?
Kerry: Not hot, probably about 20°C.
Michael: When are you 5) *leaving/leave*?
Kerry: We're flying next Monday.
Michael: Oh! 6) *Have/Do* a good trip!
Kerry: Thanks!

WRITING

1 Put Carlos's email to Heidi in the correct order.

A Guess what! I'm going to Russia with my school. We're flying to Moscow on Thursday. Then we're taking a train to St Petersburg. ___
B Hi, Heidi *1*
C Carlos ___
D I'll take lots of photos to show you. ___
E Bye for now. ___
F I'm looking forward to seeing the palaces and going on a boat trip! ___

2 Complete Marinella's email with these prepositions.

at   in x 2   on x 2   to

To: Isaac
From: Marinella
Subject: Trip to Mount Olympus

Hi Isaac,
Did you get my text? I'm going on a school trip 1) *at* the weekend. We're travelling by plane 2) ___ Athens. Then we're catching a coach to Mount Olympus 3) ___ 6 o'clock the next morning!

Mount Olympus is the highest mountain 4) ___ Greece. We're going to climb to the top. We're staying 5) ___ a hotel in a small town called Litochoro. We're coming back 6) ___ Monday. It will be amazing!
Love,
Marinella

3 You are going on holiday with your family. Write an email to your friend. In your email say where and when you are going and what you are going to do there. Remember to start and finish in a friendly way.

Revision Units 5 – 6

VOCABULARY

1 Match the conversations with these places.

> airport   ~~bus stop~~   castle   harbour
> museum   port

1 Excuse me, does the number 46 stop here?
  No, it stops further up the road, near that big tree.
  bus stop

2 So how old is this part?
  It's about three hundred years old. This was the king's bedroom.
  _____

3 Is this where your uncle keeps his fishing boat?
  Yes, it's called Boscastle. It's only a small place. There aren't many boats here.
  _____

4 What time does our plane leave?
  In about half an hour. Let's look around the shops while we're waiting.
  _____

5 It's really nice here. Is it very new?
  Yes, it's about five years old. It's got a huge collection of ancient treasure.
  _____

6 There are so many ships!
  Yes, I know. It's always busy here. I love watching the big ships arrive.
  _____

2 Complete the sentences with *in*, *at* or *on*.

1 Our train is leaving _at_ 10.29 a.m.
2 Mary Stuart was Queen of Scotland _____ the sixteenth century.
3 We'll arrive at the airport _____ two o'clock.
4 The ship called the Mary Rose sank _____ 19 July 1545.
5 I went on a yacht for the first time _____ the weekend.
6 Tom and his family are going to Mexico _____ September.
7 We moved to a house near the harbour _____ the end of last year.
8 They're catching a coach to Cardiff _____ the morning.

3 Complete the text with these words.

> caught   delay   driver   passengers   station
> tickets   train   ~~trip~~

Last month I went on a day 1) _trip_ to Manchester with my parents. We bought our train 2) _____ in Birmingham and 3) _____ a train at nine o'clock. Everything was going well and then suddenly the train stopped. After a short time the 4) _____ spoke to the 5) _____ . 'I'm afraid there is a problem with the train. I'm very sorry about the 6) _____ .' At first we didn't mind. My parents were reading their newspapers and I was listening to my MP3 player. After one hour we started to get bored. Then after two hours we really wanted to get off the 7) _____ ! At 1 o'clock we finally arrived at Manchester train 8) _____ . We didn't have a lot of time to see Manchester, but the train company gave us a free ticket because of the delay so we're going back next Saturday!

4 Choose the best answer, A, B or C.

1 It is very _dark_ inside the castle because there aren't many windows.
  (A) dark   **B** loud   **C** light
2 The *Titanic* is a very _____ ship.
  A famous   **B** ancient   **C** quiet
3 This bus isn't very _____ . There's rubbish on the floor.
  A dirty   **B** clean   **C** dangerous
4 They found some _____ inside a small box. There were gold coins and jewellery.
  A kings   **B** treasure   **C** battles
5 The _____ of Hastings happened in 1066. The fighting was between the French and the English.
  A King   **B** Castle   **C** Battle
6 Big ships make a _____ noise when they come into the port.
  A clean   **B** light   **C** loud

Revision Units 5 – 6

GRAMMAR

1 Choose the correct words.
1. The ship *who/that* took Columbus to America in 1492 was called the *Santa Maria*.
2. That's the man *which/who* drives our school bus.
3. My granddad's got a motorbike *which/who* is 85 years old.
4. Alice is the girl *which/who* found the Roman treasure.
5. My mum works in a shop *who/that* sells bicycles.
6. These are the people *which/who* arrived on the ferry yesterday.

2 Complete the sentences. Use the past simple or past continuous form of the verbs in brackets.
1. We *were sailing* (sail) to the island when my hat *fell* (fall) into the sea.
2. The train _____ (leave) the station when Jacob _____ (arrive).
3. Emma and Nathan _____ (go) to school when the tram suddenly _____ (stop).
4. Lucy _____ (get off) the ferry when she _____ (see) me.
5. I _____ (travel) around Greece in a yacht when I _____ (meet) George and Maria.
6. We _____ (play) football in the park when we _____ (hear) the helicopter.

3 Complete the short answers.
1. Are you catching the coach tonight?
   No, I *'m not* .
2. Is Tom's class studying Ancient Greece next term?
   Yes, it _____ .
3. Will you call me when you arrive?
   Yes, I _____ .
4. Are they looking for treasure?
   Yes, they _____ .
5. Is Paul going to be late?
   No, he _____ .
6. Will his daughter become queen?
   Yes, she _____ .

4 Complete the conversation with one word in each space.

William
Hurry up! The train 1) *is* leaving in 20 minutes and it 2) _____ take us 15 minutes to walk to the station.

Isobel
OK, OK! 3) _____ you taking your sunglasses with you?

William
Yes, it's 4) _____ to be hot and sunny today.

Isobel
Oh, great! I 5) _____ bring some sun cream, too. Are we going 6) _____ have a picnic at the castle?

William
No, we'll buy lunch at the café there.

Isobel
How 7) _____ we get from the station to the castle?

William
On foot, it's not far. Anyway, we 8) _____ going to be late, come on.

Isobel
All right. I'm ready now!

45

You can do it!

READING

1 Read the article. Choose which sentence fits each space. You do not need all the sentences.

> Kelly, fifteen, described the day.
> He said he couldn't stay on the board at first and that it was really funny.
> The sports centre is popular with lots of teenagers.
> ~~They are working with local schools and organising 'get sporty' days.~~
> You don't have to be good at football and basketball.
> She said you don't have to be a good dancer and it's lots of fun.

Do you love or hate sport?

Certainly some teens love sport, but for others sport is not fun at all. One sports centre is trying to change this. The staff at Mayfield Sports Centre believe that everyone can find a sport they enjoy. 1) _They are working with local schools and organising 'get sporty' days_. These 'get sporty' days give teenagers the chance to try different kinds of sports. Freegrove Secondary School had a 'get sporty' day last month and I went to talk to some of the students.
2) _____ She explained that there were twelve different sports, for example, gymnastics, judo, dance and volleyball. Every thirty minutes the students had to move round to the next sport. Rosie, fourteen, really enjoyed the day. She loved the dance lesson and now goes to a zumba dance class every Wednesday.
3) _____ Another Freegrove student, Adam, tried skateboarding. 4) _____ Adam doesn't like sport at school very much – you know, football and basketball – but he thinks skateboarding's cool.

2 Read the article and choose the best title.
1 Why teens love sport
2 Teens get sporty!
3 New sports centre opens at Freegrove School

VOCABULARY
Sports and equipment

1 Find and write six sports.

g	i	n	f	o	n	s	t	e	s	a	g
s	h	o	r	s	e	r	i	d	i	n	g
o	n	t	i	n	g	d	i	d	i	n	b
n	t	o	g	f	d	e	s	d	i	n	a
p	e	n	t	s	w	e	r	o	k	i	s
l	n	a	i	e	n	a	o	j	o	o	k
g	n	i	n	n	o	n	b	u	s	h	e
s	i	n	t	b	e	e	n	d	o	n	t
i	s	w	e	r	e	d	i	o	n	a	b
s	a	t	b	a	l	i	s	k	o	l	a
a	i	n	r	u	n	n	i	n	g	x	l
k	o	n	b	a	s	k	y	b	a	i	l

1 _horse-riding_   2 _____
3 _____   4 _____
5 _____   6 _____

2 Choose the correct answer, A, B or C.
1 Why have you got that racket with you?
   A I've got a tennis lesson after school.
   B I'm playing in a basketball match later.
   C I'm going swimming with my sister.
2 Have you got any goggles I can borrow?
   A No, sorry, I don't play football.
   B Yes, I'll bring them to the swimming pool.
   C Yes, I have to wear them for gymnastics.
3 Isn't it a bit cold for surfing today, Jane?
   A Don't worry, Mum, I'll wear goggles.
   B Don't worry, Mum, I'll wear a swimsuit.
   C Don't worry, Mum, I'll wear a wetsuit.
4 Why can't we play volleyball today?
   A The board's broken.
   B The net's broken.
   C The helmet's broken.

07 You can do it!

5 Is that a new board, Gina?
  A Yes, I'm going to the gym now.
  B Yes, I'm going to the swimming pool now.
  C Yes, I'm going to the skateboarding park now.
6 Can I go horse-riding with Ella, Mum?
  A OK, but don't forget your helmet.
  B OK, but don't forget your ball.
  C OK, but don't forget your net.

3 Complete the sentences. Use the correct form of these expressions.

> do synchronised swimming   ~~play football~~
> go cycling   go skiing   do gymnastics
> play volleyball

1 She _plays football._

2 He _____

3 She _____

4 He _____

5 She _____

6 He _____

4 Choose the correct words.
1 Nick *plays/does* judo every Tuesday after school.
2 I *played/did* volleyball on the beach with my friends at the weekend.
3 Do you want to *go/do* gymnastics or go on the sports field?
4 I'm *doing/going* surfing with my sister after lunch.
5 My dad *goes/plays* running every morning at 6.30.
6 We *played/went* horse-riding when we were on holiday.
7 Kelly *goes/plays* skateboarding in the park at the weekends.
8 They're going to *go/play* basketball at school tomorrow.

5 Complete the advert with the correct words.

Archway Activity Centre
We have an activity for everyone here at Archway.

For people who like the outdoors, we have
1) _horse-riding_ for all levels and ages.
There are also lots of team games such as football and 2) _____.
Other outdoor activities include
3) _____,
4) _____ and
5) _____.
When the weather is bad, we have great indoor activities to offer.

Why not try 6) _____ or
7) _____?
Our teachers are friendly and helpful.
We hope to see you soon at Archway!

See our website for more information – www.archway.activity.centre.

6 Complete the table with the correct verbs.

cycling	1) *cycle*
skiing	2) _____
surfing	3) _____
skateboarding	4) _____
running	5) _____
swimming	6) _____
climbing	7) _____

7 Complete the sentences with these words.

> ~~climbed~~   cycle   ran   skied
> surfed   swam

1 We had lunch after we *climbed* to the top of the rock.
2 They took their boards to the beach and _____ all morning.
3 Now I have a new bike I _____ to school every morning.
4 Robbie _____ from the boat to the island.
5 Chloe _____ the fastest and won the 100 m race.
6 We _____ really fast down the mountain – it was great fun!

8 Choose the correct words.

Hi Marta
My school is great for sports. Every week we have two PE lessons. In the summer, we usually 1) **go/play** tennis and volleyball. In the winter, we often 2) **play/do** gymnastics. There are also lots of after-school clubs. On Mondays there is volleyball 3) **practice/play** and on Tuesday there is a 4) **basketball/swimming** club at the local pool. I go to the football club on Wednesdays. I 5) **do/play** for the school girls' football team. Every year we have a skiing trip to France. I went last year and 6) **skiing/skied** for the first time – I loved it! Our history teacher 7) **does/plays** judo and he's going to start a club next month. I really want to go to that club.
Love, Kim x

GRAMMAR
Ability, possibility and obligation

1 Complete the sentences. Use *can* or *can't* and the verb in brackets.

1 Ruby *can't swim* (swim). She's afraid of water.
2 My parents _____ (ride) a bike. They go cycling in the mountains.
3 Mark and Karen _____ (surf). They take their boards to the beach every weekend.
4 I _____ (skateboard). I tried it once, but I fell off all the time. I didn't enjoy it.
5 Lily _____ (run) very fast. She won a competition last month.
6 William _____ (play) tennis. He started lessons when he was just six years old.

2 Make questions with *can*. Then complete the short answers.

1 your sister / ski / ?
Can your sister ski?
No, *she can't.*
2 you / do / gymnastics / ?
_____
No, _____
3 Mark / play / volleyball / ?
_____
Yes, _____
4 Amelia and Eve / swim / ?
_____
Yes, _____
5 Max / ride / bike / ?
_____
No, _____
6 your parents / skateboard / ?
_____
No, _____

07 You can do it!

3 Complete the sentences with *can*, *can't*, *could* or *couldn't*.

Harriet: I remember the first time I went surfing. I 1) *couldn't* stay on the board! 2) .... you surf?

Ben: Yes, I 3) .... I go surfing with my brothers in the summer.

Jane: 4) .... you play tennis when you were five?

Liam: No, I 5) .... , but I learnt to play when I was seven.

Dean: 6) .... you ski, Nick?

Nick: No, I 7) .... , but I'm going for the first time this December. I 8) .... skateboard so I think it will be easy to learn.

Kyle: 9) .... you swim when you were six?

Will: Yes, I 10) .... I learnt to swim when I was very young.

4 Complete the text with the best answer, A, B or C, for each space.

Racing Club
Tuesdays, 4.30 p.m. @ the race track

1) *Can* you ride a bike? Do you enjoy cycling 2) .... ? Then why not join our club?

You 3) .... have to wear special clothing, just something warm and some trainers. You 4) .... wear a helmet because it 5) .... be dangerous.

Racing club is £3 a week but you 6) .... come the first week free of charge.

We hope to see you soon!

*You 7) .... be over 14 years old to join the club.

1	**A** Could	**(B)** Can	**C** Can't
2	**A** fast	**B** faster	**C** fastest
3	**A** don't	**B** didn't	**C** doesn't
4	**A** had to	**B** has to	**C** have to
5	**A** can	**B** can't	**C** couldn't
6	**A** can't	**B** couldn't	**C** can
7	**A** have to	**B** has to	**C** had to

5 Complete the sentences with *have to/has to* or *don't have to/doesn't have to*.

1 Rebecca *has to* wear a helmet when she goes horse-riding.
2 You .... wear goggles when you go skiing, but it's a good idea.
3 Tom .... miss basketball practice today because he's ill.
4 We .... do gymnastics at school, but I choose to do it.
5 Sometimes they .... finish tennis matches early because of rain.
6 Mathew and Clara .... cycle to school because their mum doesn't have a car.

6 Match the questions (1–6) with the answers (A–F).

1 Do we have to wear goggles in the pool? *F*
2 Did Aaron have to play in the basketball match?
3 Does everyone have to wear a cycling helmet?
4 Can your mum ski well?
5 Do I have to wear trainers for judo?
6 Could Mark kiteboard last summer?

A Yes, he did. The team captain was sick.
B Yes, she can. She won lots of skiing competitions when she was young.
C No, you don't. You don't wear anything on your feet.
D Yes, they do. It can be dangerous when they're cycling very fast.
E No, he couldn't. He only learnt to do it this year.
F No, you don't have to, but the water can make your eyes red.

7 Complete the text with one word in each space.

Local girl number 1 in gymnastics competition!

Samantha Combe is a very happy 14-year-old. Yesterday, she won a national gymnastics competition. She 1) _had_ to practise very hard for the competition. Every day she had to 2) _____ four hours of gymnastics. She didn't have 3) _____ go far to practise – Samantha lives next door to the gym! The competition was very difficult and she 4) _____ to beat ten other girls to win first prize. Today Samantha is relaxing at home with a DVD. She 5) _____ have to practise for a few days so she 6) _____ have a rest!

Adverbs

8 Complete the sentences with adverbs formed from the adjectives in brackets.

1 He plays tennis _well_ . (good)
2 Clare runs _____ . (fast)
3 David always arrives _____ . (late)
4 I play football _____ . (bad)
5 She won the race _____ . (easy)
6 She climbed up the mountain _____ . (slow)

LISTENING

1 🔊 **7.1 Listen to five conversations. Choose the correct answer, A, B or C.**

1 What time is the basketball match? _A_
2 What did Marcia get for her birthday? ___
3 What is Martin's favourite sport? ___
4 What did Karen buy at the sports shop? ___
5 Where is Liam's sports bag? ___

2 🔊 **7.2 Listen again and choose the correct answers.**

1 The two boys are going to meet _at the gym_/in the park.
2 The skateboard belongs to Marcia's brother/friend.
3 The judo club is in the morning/after school.
4 Karen is going surfing tomorrow/next weekend.
5 Liam's mother is washing some clothes/the car.

07 You can do it!

SPEAKING SKILLS

1 Match the places (1–6) with the signs (A–F).

1 library __A__
2 shop _____
3 swimming pool _____
4 airport _____
5 zoo _____
6 road _____

2 Choose the correct answers.

1 **A** What does that sign mean?
  B It means that we *can't swim here/can swim here/don't have to swim here*.
2 **A** What does this sign mean?
  B It *mean/means/meant* we can't skateboard here.
3 **A** Do you know what the sign means?
  B *I'm not sure/I don't sure/I'm not surely* but I think it means 'no running'.
4 **A** Is the sports centre open?
  B No. The sign *is saying/say/says* it's closed.
5 **A** Do you know what that sign means?
  B *Yes/it means that you can/have to/can't* play other sports here.

WRITING

1 Read about Samantha and complete the profile with *too*, *also* and *as well*.

This month's tennis star
Samantha Mae Coyiuto

There isn't much that Samantha Mae Coyiuto can't do! She started playing tennis when she was eight and won her first national competition when she was ten. Samantha works hard. She trains six times a week and has to find time for her homework 1) __as well__. She loves tennis, but thinks swimming and badminton are fun, 2) _____. She says sport is important because we learn that we can't win all the time.

Sport isn't the only thing that Samantha does well. She's 3) _____ a writer and has fantastic ideas for her books about teenagers. When she was sixteen, Samantha wrote *Flight to the Stars*, her first book for young adults. When Samantha has free time, she 4) _____ likes chatting to her friends.

2 Read the notes and complete the profile with one word for each space.

Quillan Isidore
Sport: BMX
From: South London
Age 8: started cycling
Age 15: won U16 BMX world championship at National Indoor Arena in Birmingham
Training: 2 hours after school + 4–5 hours at weekend
Dream: race in Olympic Games

Quillan Isidore is a 1) __BMX__ rider from South 2) _____. He started 3) _____ when he was eight, when a friend took him to a local BMX track. On 26 May 2012, fifteen-year-old Quillan became the U16 BMX 4) _____ champion at the National Indoor Arena in Birmingham. He beat Cristobal Palominos from Chile and Sean Gaian from the USA. Quillan does two hours of training after 5) _____ and then another four to five hours at the weekends when he's not racing. His dream is to race in the 6) _____ Games.

3 Write about your favourite sport or hobby. Say when you started it, when and where you do it and who you do it with.

08 See the world

READING

1 Read the article and choose right (R), wrong (W) or doesn't say (DS) for each sentence.

> 'Mom, I'm calling you from the top of the world!'
>
> This is what Jordan Romero said to his mother when he phoned her from the top of Mount Everest. Jordan was only thirteen years old and the youngest person to climb the highest mountain in the world.
>
> Jordan is from Big Bear Lake in California and he and his family love climbing mountains. Everest is not the only mountain Jordan has climbed. He has now completed the 'Seven Summits'. What are the Seven Summits? They are the highest mountains of each of the seven continents. Most of us have only seen these mountains in books or on TV, but Jordan Romero has stood at the top of each of them! He climbed Mount Kilimanjaro in Africa when he was only ten. He climbed the last of the seven summits in 2011 when he was fifteen. This was Vinson Massif in Antarctica.
>
> Jordan became interested in climbing these mountains one day at school. He saw a painting of the Seven Summits in the school hall. He decided then that he wanted to see these mountains for himself.
>
> He has written a book with Katherine Blanc about climbing Everest. The book is full of photos of his expedition. Jordan hopes that other teenagers will read about his adventures and it will make them follow their dreams.

1 Jordan's mother was with him at the top of Everest. _W_
2 Jordan's family loves lakes. ____
3 Jordan has climbed all of the Seven Summits. ____
4 Mount Everest was the first mountain Jordan climbed. ____

2 Read the article again and answer the questions. Write short answers.

1 How old was Jordan when he climbed Mount Everest? _thirteen years old_
2 Where is Bear Lake? ____
3 How many continents has Jordan visited? ____
4 When did Jordan climb Vinson Massif in Antarctica? ____
5 Who does Jordan hope will read his book? ____

VOCABULARY
The natural world

1 Find and write the names of eight animals.

s	u	o	m	o	o	n	s	t	z
t	g	r	o	e	h	a	n	d	a
a	i	e	u	z	e	a	a	a	r
k	r	e	s	n	h	i	k	e	d
e	a	n	e	p	d	e	e	t	y
e	f	f	e	r	i	g	r	i	f
t	f	l	o	n	e	d	i	g	s
l	e	o	p	a	r	d	e	e	x
u	d	o	r	i	z	e	b	r	a
n	g	u	l	e	b	r	i	d	e

1 _mouse_   2 _____
3 _____   4 _____
5 _____   6 _____
7 _____   8 _____

2 Find and write six adjectives.

asddsfdifficultaseddgreatasddfunaadssascaryasdfdexcitingasddlonelydsdfg

1 _difficult_   2 _____
3 _____   4 _____
5 _____   6 _____

08 See the world

3 Choose the correct words.

1. How was your elephant ride?
   Great!/*Scary*! I loved it. The elephant was very friendly and gentle.
2. Did you finish your homework about spiders?
   Not all of it. I found it really *difficult*/*lonely*.
3. What did you think of the safari?
   It was really *lonely*/*exciting* and my friends loved it, too.
4. Do you enjoy filming leopards in China?
   Yes, I do, but it can be *fun*/*lonely* sometimes and I miss my family.
5. Was your trip to the zoo *difficult*/*fun*?
   Yes, we really enjoyed it.
6. Why don't you like spiders? They're really cute!
   No, they're not! They're really *scary*/*great*!

4 Choose the correct words or phrases.

1. It was *freezing cold*/*cool* yesterday. It was –3°C when we walked to school!
2. We'd like a *hot*/*cool* drink, please. It's boiling hot outside!
3. Would you like another blanket or are you *warm*/*cold* enough?
4. Don't touch the water, it's *warm*/*boiling hot*. You'll hurt your hand.
5. We'll have *cold*/*cool* food at the party. I'll make some salads and sandwiches.
6. It's very *hot*/*cool* in here. Can we open a window, please?

5 Complete the sentences with the correct weather adjectives.

> cloudy foggy ~~rainy~~ snowy
> stormy sunny windy

1. I always take my umbrella when it's ____rainy____.
2. When it's very _____ we go skiing in the mountains.
3. It's a really _____ day. Let's go to the beach!
4. Why are you wearing sunglasses? It's _____ .
5. It's very _____ . It's great weather for flying kites!
6. We can't sail our boat when it's _____ . It's too dangerous.
7. They can't see the top of the mountain because it's _____ .

6 Test your geography! Match the places (1–7) with the correct continents (a–g).

1. Brazil
2. Egypt
3. Canada
4. China
5. The South Pole
6. New Zealand
7. Poland

a. Asia
b. Europe
c. South America
d. Antarctica
e. Australia
f. Africa
g. North America

7 Complete the crossword.

Across

3. water that travels across land to the sea
5. a very high area of land
7. a large area of water that has and all around it
8. a very large sea
9. a very dry place with lots of sand
10. a small area with trees

Down

1. a place with lots of very tall trees where it often rains
2. a place with lots of trees
4. a high area of land smaller than 5 across
6. a place with water all around it

8 Complete the sentences with these measurements.

> 53 kg   6,650 km   8 cm   ~~2°C~~   300 kg

1 It's only ____2°C____. It's very cold today.
2 The River Nile is _____ long.
3 This Siberian tiger weighs _____ .
4 My pet mouse is _____ long.
5 My friend Joshua weighs _____ .

9 Complete the conversation with these words.

> Asia   continents   spring   summer
> temperature   weather   winter   ~~world~~

Martin: Hi. I'm Martin from *Teen Travel* magazine and we're talking to teenagers from different cities around the 1) ____world____ . What's your name and where do you come from?
Leyla: Hi. I'm Leyla and I come from Istanbul in Turkey.
Martin: So what's interesting about your city?
Leyla: Well, Istanbul's unusual because it's in two 2) _____ . The old part of the city is in Europe and the new part of the city is in 3) _____ .
Martin: That is unusual! What's the 4) _____ like in your city?
Leyla: It changes at different times of the year. In Istanbul 5) _____ starts in June and finishes in September. July is usually the warmest month. The 6) _____ once reached 37°C, but it isn't usually that hot. It's normally around 28°C.
Martin: And does it get cold in Istanbul?
Leyla: It doesn't really start to get cold until the middle of December. It usually snows in 7) _____ . The weather starts to get warmer again in March when 8) _____ starts.

GRAMMAR
Present perfect simple

1 Complete the sentences with the correct form of *have*. Use the contractions *'ve/'s* where possible.

1 **Joel:** Did you enjoy your trip to Venezuela?
  Connie: Yes, we loved it.
  Joel: Was it your first trip to South America?
  Connie: No, we __'ve__ been there before.
2 **Dad:** How do you know so much about the South Pole, Kerry?
  Kerry: We _____ read lots of books about Antarctica at school, Dad.
3 **Sara:** How did you find this beach? It's amazing!
  Anna: Mark and Kerry _____ been here before. They told me about it.
4 **Mark:** Does Richard know lots of people here?
  Noah: Yes, he _____ visited this island many times. A lot of people on the island know him now.
5 **William:** Do you like mountain climbing?
  Olivia: I love it! I _____ climbed the highest mountain in my country.
6 **Kate:** Where is Andrea going next month?
  Nick: Kenya and Tanzania. She _____ travelled to Asia and Europe and now she wants to go to Africa.

2 Put the words in the correct order to make negative sentences and questions.

1 hasn't / Jacob / my pet snake / seen / .
  Jacob hasn't seen my pet snake.
2 a zoo / you / Have / been / ever / to/ ?

3 never / by boat / travelled / We've / .

4 ever / to Tokyo / Charlotte / Has / been / ?

5 a holiday / They / had / in the UK / haven't / .

6 it / here / Has / snowed / ever / ?

54 GOLD EXPERIENCE

08 See the world

3 Complete the table with the past participles of the verbs.

go	1) been/gone
see	2)
take	3)
buy	4)
read	5)
catch	6)
teach	7)

4 Complete the sentences with the present perfect form of the verbs in brackets.

1 Eric _has stayed_ (stay) in many places in Thailand.
2 Jimmy and Didier _____ (see) a tiger in the wild.
3 Harriet _____ (not be) to Europe before.
4 This is the first time it _____ (snow) here.
5 We _____ (not buy) our tickets to Italy yet.
6 I _____ (not hold) a snake before.

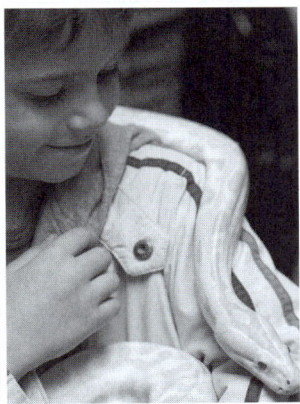

5 Complete the short answers.

1 Have you ever been to Australia?
   No, _I haven't_ .
2 Has Tracy read the book about Antarctica?
   Yes, _____ .
3 Have they camped in a desert before?
   No, _____ .
4 Has it snowed here before?
   No, _____ .
5 Have Ben and Kerry skied in these mountains?
   Yes, _____ .
6 Has your granddad ever lived on another continent?
   Yes, _____ .

LISTENING

1 🔊 8.1 Listen to a conversation. Who are the two people? Choose the correct answer.
1 two friends
2 a teacher and a student
3 a father and a daughter

2 🔊 8.2 Listen again and choose the correct answer, A, B or C.
1 What was Amy's last geography project about?
   A lakes
   B rivers
   Ⓒ mountains
2 Where are Amy's photos from?
   A her teacher
   B a magazine
   C the Internet
3 Which river has Amy's dad seen?
   A the Mississippi
   B the Amazon
   C the Nile
4 How long is Lake Victoria?
   A 322 km
   B 320 km
   C 332 km
5 When does the rainy season start at Lake Victoria?
   A April
   B March
   C May
6 How low can the night temperature be at Lake Victoria in June?
   A 15°C
   B 10°C
   C 2°C

55

GRAMMAR
Using *ever* and *never* with the present perfect

1 Make questions. Use the present perfect with *ever*.

1 you / see / a black widow spider / ?
   Have you ever seen a black widow spider?
2 your teacher / be / to the Amazon / ?
3 your parents / be / mountain climbing / ?
4 Georgina / sleep / in a rainforest / ?
5 they / find / a mouse in their house / ?
6 Martin / visit / the island of Corsica / ?

2 Make sentences with *never*. Use the present perfect form of these verbs.

| climb live rain ride see ~~swim~~ |

1 Mark *has never swum* in an ocean.
2 Susan and Matthew _____ a mountain.
3 It _____ in this part of the desert.
4 My sister _____ on an elephant, but it's something she really wants to do.
5 This snake _____ in the wild. It was born in the zoo.
6 Lucien _____ fog before. They don't have fog in his country.

3 Complete the text with the best answer, A, B or C, in each space.

Adventureholiday4u.com

Katie is a lucky 14-year-old. She has 1) *travelled* all over the world with her parents, Mandy and Tom. We asked Katie to talk to us about some of her adventure holidays.
— How many adventure holidays 2) _____ you been on?
— Six. I 3) _____ on my first adventure holiday when I was seven.
— Wow! Have you got a favourite holiday?
— Not really. I've 4) _____ all the holidays. I love animals so our last holiday was fantastic — we went on safari in Tanzania.
— Have you 5) _____ had a scary experience on one of your adventure holidays?
— Yes. When we were on safari in Tanzania an elephant ran towards our jeep. That was scary, but also amazing!
— What kinds of sports or activities have you 6) _____ on holiday?
— Well, my family loves extreme sports. We've been ice climbing in Canada, snowboarding in the desert in Dubai and surfing in Australia.
— Fantastic! So why do you like adventure holidays so much?
— You're never bored! I've 7) _____ lots of amazing places and done brilliant things on my holidays. I've 8) _____ been on a beach holiday — and I don't want to! I love adventure holidays!

1 A travelling   **B travelled**   C travels
2 A have   B has   C had
3 A go   B went   C gone
4 A enjoy   B enjoying   C enjoyed
5 A ever   B never   C not
6 A do   B did   C done
7 A see   B seen   C saw
8 A ever   B never   C not

08 See the world

SPEAKING SKILLS

1 Put the words in the correct order.

1 you / are / doing / ? / What / at the weekend
   What are you doing at the weekend?
2 you / camping / been / before / ? / Have
3 are / you / ? / Where / going
4 your bikes / ? / Are / taking / with you / you
5 fishing / never / I / been / . / 've
6 time / Have / good / ! / a

2 Read the conversation. Choose which sentence fits each space. You do not need all the sentences.

> Thanks, you too! See you on Monday.
> Yes, we've all got mountain bikes. I think we'll go fishing, too.
> We're going to a campsite in Dark River Forest.
> Never? Do you want to come with us this weekend?
> Have you been camping in this forest?
> I don't like fish very much.
> ~~I'm going camping with my cousins.~~
> No, this will be my first time. Have you?

Ella: Hi, Simon. What are you doing at the weekend?
Simon: 1) *I'm going camping with my cousins.*
Ella: Have you been camping before?
Simon: 2)
Ella: Yes, I go every summer. It's great fun! Where are you going?
Simon: 3)
Ella: I've been there. It's cool! Are you taking your bikes with you?
Simon: 4)
Ella: That sounds good. I've never been fishing.
Simon: 5)
Ella: Thanks, but I can't. I'm visiting my grandparents. Well, have a good time!
Simon: 6)

WRITING

1 Complete the postcard with these words.

boat   city   ~~Scotland~~   fog   yesterday   highest

Hi Jack,
I'm having a great time in Scotland. We've travelled to lots of brilliant places. We started in Edinburgh, the capital of 1) *Scotland* . I love Edinburgh. It has an amazing castle in the middle of the 2) _____ . We've also been to the Highlands. We went mountain biking on Ben Nevis, Great Britain's 3) _____ mountain. That was really exciting – and a bit scary! We went to Loch Ness 4) _____ . We went on a 5) _____ trip, but we didn't see the monster!
The weather is very strange here. We have had sun, rain and 6) _____ – and it has snowed!
See you soon,
Leah

2 Write the adjectives Leah uses in her postcard to describe these things.

1 her time in Scotland – *great*
2 the places she has travelled to – _____
3 Edinburgh Castle – _____
4 mountain biking on Ben Nevis – _____ and _____
5 the weather in Scotland – _____

3 You are on a school trip. Write a postcard to a friend. Write about where you are, the activities and the weather. Use adjectives to make your postcard interesting and remember to begin and end in a friendly way.

Revision Units 7 – 8

VOCABULARY

1 Choose the correct words.
1 Have you ever *played*/been volleyball on a beach?
2 Has Andrew ever *been*/*played* cycling with you?
3 Have you ever *done*/*been* gymnastics at school?
4 Has Sarah ever *played*/*done* synchronised swimming?
5 Has Michael ever *been*/*played* skiing in France?
6 Has Simon ever *done*/*played* football for the school team?

2 Choose the correct words.
1 Martin swam to the other side of the *lake*/*ocean* really fast.
2 We love playing in the *rainforest*/*wood* near our house. It's great in the winter when it snows.
3 I'm really good at running. I can run up that *mountain*/*hill* in ten minutes.
4 We always go to this *island*/*desert* on holiday. It's always hot and sunny and it's so green.
5 I've never been to the top of a *forest*/*mountain* because I don't like heights.
6 Juliette and her dad like going fishing in the *river*/*island*.

3 Complete the sentences with these words.

> board ~~goggles~~ helmet net rackets swimsuits

1 *Goggles* can help you see better when you swim underwater.
2 Do you want to go surfing? You don't need to have your own _____ .
3 Do you want to play tennis? I've got two _____ .
4 It's so hot and sunny. Let's put on our _____ and go to the beach.
5 Cycling in the mountains can be dangerous so you have to wear a _____ .
6 The volleyball _____ has a big hole in it. Can you fix it for us, please?

4 Complete the conversation with these words.

> cool fast ~~freezing~~ kiteboarding snow sunny wetsuits windy

Daniel
Hi, Maria. How was your trip to the mountains?

Maria
Good, thanks. It was 1) *freezing* cold, though!

Daniel
Did it 2) _____ ?

Maria
Yes, a lot. We went skiing every day. How about your trip? Where did you go?

Daniel
Crete, in Greece. It was great. It was really 3) _____ .

Maria
Did you go in the sea?

Daniel
Yes, but the water was a bit 4) _____ so we wore 5) _____ . We also tried 6) _____ on the beach.

Maria
Wow! I've never done that.

Daniel
It was my first time. It was very 7) _____ so we went really 8) _____ . It was great!

Revision Units 7 – 8

GRAMMAR

1 Complete the sentences with adverbs formed from the adjectives in brackets.

1 The giraffes moved _slowly_ in the hot weather. (slow)
2 The elephant hurt its foot and was walking _____ . (bad)
3 We couldn't hear the snake. It moved _____ through the rainforest. (quiet)
4 The mouse escaped _____ through the small hole in the wall. (easy)
5 Leopards are good at climbing. They can climb trees really _____ . (good)
6 Tigers can run very _____ – often 35 miles an hour. (fast)

2 Complete the conversations with the present perfect form of these verbs.

climb ~~cycle~~ be run skateboard wear

1 _Have_ you ever _cycled_ through a forest?
Yes, I have. I took my bike when I visited Sherwood Forest.
2 _____ Mark ever _____ a tree?
Yes, he has. When he was young he had a tree house.
3 _____ your dad ever _____ ?
Yes, he has. He tried on my board, but he fell off lots of times!
4 _____ they ever _____ to Africa?
Yes, they have. They went to Morocco last September.
5 _____ you ever _____ a wetsuit?
Yes, I have. I went surfing in the UK and the sea was freezing cold!
6 _____ Rachel ever _____ in a race?
Yes, she has. She did the New York marathon last year. Her feet really hurt afterwards!

3 Choose the correct answer, A, B or C.

1 Jake _couldn't swim_ when he started at our school, but now he's a really good swimmer.
  A had to swim
  B couldn't swim
  C has swum

2 David _____ snow before. He comes from Botswana in Africa.
  A has never seen
  B can see
  C has to see
3 You _____ lessons to learn how to surf, but it's a good idea.
  A can't take
  B don't have to take
  C couldn't take
4 Horse-riding _____ dangerous so I always wear a helmet.
  A can be
  B has to be
  C couldn't be
5 I _____ to Europe, but I would like to go one day.
  A could be
  B had to be
  C haven't been
6 We _____ tennis at the moment because there isn't a net.
  A can't play
  B have to play
  C have played

4 Complete the conversation. Use one word in each space.

Paul: Have you 1) _ever_ been to Blackwood Activity Centre?
Holly: 2) _____ , I haven't. What can you do there?
Paul: Lots of things. You 3) _____ do horse-riding, kiteboarding, rock climbing and judo.
Holly: So, 4) _____ you been there?
Paul: Yes, I went last Saturday.
Holly: What 5) _____ you do?
Paul: I wanted to go kiteboarding, but we couldn't because it was too windy.
Holly: I thought it has 6) _____ be windy for kiteboarding.
Paul: It does, but when it's very windy it can 7) _____ dangerous. I did judo instead – I really enjoyed it.
Holly: Yes, I love judo. I go to a judo club at the sports centre.
Paul: 8) _____ you have to be good to join the club?
Holly: No, you don't. Why don't you come with me next time?

09 Let me entertain you

READING

1 Read the film review and comments. Answer the questions. Write short answers.

My_favourite_DVD_film.com

Hi. My name's Zack and my favourite film is Frankenweenie. I've loved the director, Tim Burton, since I was eleven, when I saw another of his films, Charlie and the Chocolate Factory. Tim Burton has directed over fifteen films since 1982, but I think Frankenweenie is the best. It is a black and white animation. The story is about a schoolboy called Victor Frankenstein and his dog, Sparky. Victor is good at science and he loves making machines and filming movies about monsters. One day, a car hits Sparky and he dies. Victor is very sad and makes a machine to bring Sparky back to life. For me, the first half of the film is the best. It's really funny and there are some really good jokes. There are lots of funny and interesting characters like Weird Girl. I think this is a really great animation and I give it 9/10.

What do you think?

Tom, 14: I've been a fan of Tim Burton's animations for years, but I thought this film was boring!

Maria, 15: I thought Frankenweenie was great. Last year my favourite Tim Burton film was Alice in Wonderland, but this is my favourite now!

Rosalind, 14: I've watched this lots of times and it always makes me laugh, but I don't understand why the film is in black and white – very annoying!

---

1 How old was Zack when he watched Charlie and the Chocolate Factory? _eleven_
2 How many films has Tim Burton directed since 1982?
3 What's the name of Victor Frankenstein's dog?
4 What does Victor like to make films about?
5 What adjective does Tom use to describe the film?
6 What is Maria's favourite Tim Burton film?

2 Find words in the film review that match these meanings.

1 best liked or most enjoyed: _favourite_
2 someone who tells the actors in a film what to do: d
3 the study of natural things: s
4 unhappy: s
5 50% of something: h
6 the people in a film: c

VOCABULARY
Entertainment

1 Match the types of TV shows (1–6) with the programmes (A–F) in the TV guide.

1 talent show — _B_
2 chat show
3 news programme
4 documentary
5 soap opera
6 sports programme

19.00	**A Cat watch** Michelle Oldfield follows a family of tigers in Cambodia.
19.30	**B Star lights** Who will win the competition? Will it be Sandy the magician, Denzel the singer or the dancing group Fire? Find out tonight.
20.30	**C Harvey Street** In tonight's episode, find out whether Amy left Mark – and is Robert telling the truth about the accident?
21.00	**D Points East** Find out what's happening in your area.
21.15	**E Talk with Tina** The actor Mark Robson is a guest on Tina's show tonight. He will talk about his new film.
22.00	**F Match Round Up** All the results from today's matches and races.

09 Let me entertain you

2 Complete the sentences.
1. An _actor_ is someone who acts.
2. A _____ is someone who dances.
3. A _____ is someone who sings.
4. A _____ is someone who does magic tricks.
5. A _____ is someone who plays music.
6. A _____ is someone who performs comedy.
7. A _____ is someone who wears funny clothes and makes children laugh.
8. An _____ is a girl or woman who acts.

3 Choose the correct words.
1. My sister loves <u>soap operas</u>/sports programmes. Her favourite is about a family called the Fletchers.
2. I love singing and dancing. One day I want to go on a documentary/talent show.
3. Some actors are very private and they never go on chat shows/sports programmes.
4. My dad's on the sports programme/news programme at 6 o'clock. They interviewed him about his business.
5. My brother watches a sports programme/chat show every Saturday evening. He's mad about football.
6. I saw a really interesting documentary/soap opera about Machu Picchu last night.

4 Put the letters in order to make different types of films.
1. icatno ilmf — _action film_
2. niomaatin — _____
3. odcyme — _____
4. oorrrh lfmi — _____
5. mcraonti mfli — _____
6. icseenc iftcnio ifml — _____

5 Choose the correct words.
1. I love this romantic/<u>science fiction</u> film. It's about a man who saves the world from aliens.
2. This horror film/comedy is really funny. You won't stop laughing!
3. I'm not interested in action/comedy films. They're full of fighting and fast cars.
4. My brother doesn't like romantic/action films. He doesn't like any films about love.
5. This animation/horror film is about the characters from my favourite comic. It's great fun!
6. I don't like watching romantic/horror films before I go to sleep because they give me scary dreams.

6 Find and write six adjectives to describe films or TV shows.

b	o	r	i	n	f	s	c	a	s
i	n	g	n	i	g	u	n	k	c
n	o	l	t	e	r	e	n	s	a
g	i	s	e	l	l	i	o	n	r
o	b	o	r	i	n	g	k	r	y
n	g	n	e	t	r	s	i	o	n
r	i	d	s	t	r	a	n	g	e
o	u	s	t	c	a	n	y	o	u
r	i	d	i	c	u	l	o	u	s
f	u	i	n	t	e	r	i	n	g
y	a	r	g	o	g	e	t	s	o

1. _scary_
2. _____
3. _____
4. _____
5. _____
6. _____

7 Choose the best answer, A, B or C.
1. We saw a really _funny_ comedian on TV last night. We couldn't stop laughing.
   A scary   B boring   **C** funny
2. Harry is a great _____. He can play the guitar and the drums.
   A magician   B musician   C singer
3. The magician was wearing a _____ hat with a pineapple on top of it!
   A ridiculous   B scary   C boring
4. Tom's a great _____. He was in a really scary horror film.
   A comedian   B magician   C actor
5. Did you watch that _____ 'Gold'? I think the stories are always ridiculous.
   A news programme
   B soap opera
   C talent show
6. The Great Alfonso was a famous _____. He did some brilliant card tricks.
   A magician   B dancer   C singer

8 Complete the text with these words.

audience   comedian   contestants   judges
show   stage   ~~talent show~~   TV

Reach for the Stars! is a new
1) _talent show_ that is starting on Channel 9
next week. There are many talent shows on
2) _____ , but this one is different as it
is only for teenagers. All the 3) _____
are between 14 and 19 years old. They will
perform on 4) _____ in front of four
5) _____ who will be a dancer, a singer,
a 6) _____ and a magician. The judges
will give the contestants marks out of ten, but
the 7) _____ will decide which contestant
leaves the 8) _____ each week. It starts
next Thursday. Don't miss it!

GRAMMAR
Present perfect with *for* and *since*

1 Put the words in the correct order to make sentences.

1 played / Cathy / in the band / for six months / has / .
  Cathy has played in the band for six months.
2 since 1988 / has / on TV / been / This soap opera / .
3 loved / since she was a small child / ballet dancing / has / Michaela / .
4 have / for two years / had / Theo and Robin / singing lessons / .
5 played / since I was eight years old / 've / the violin / I / .
6 our drama teacher / known / We / for a long time / 've / .

2 Choose the correct word, *for* or *since*.

1 for/<u>since</u> this morning
2 for/since three hours
3 for/since ages
4 for/since yesterday
5 for/since twelve weeks
6 for/since 1931
7 for/since the twelfth century
8 for/since a few minutes

3 Choose the correct words.

1 We've been here *since/for* 3 o'clock.
2 Maria Cohen has appeared in this soap opera *since/for* thirteen years.
3 My cousin's been a professional ballet dancer *since/for* she was sixteen.
4 I've been interested in magic *since/for* I was a small child.
5 Colette has been a musician *since/for* a long time.
6 They have won lots of talent competitions *since/for* they started their band.

09 Let me entertain you

4 Complete the sentences. Use the present perfect form of the verbs in brackets and *for* or *since*.

1. Sara *has had* her guitar *since* her thirteenth birthday. (have)
2. I _____ to the cinema _____ a long time. (not be)
3. Joe _____ as a professional clown _____ ten years. (work)
4. Diane _____ that actor _____ his first film in 2007. (love)
5. They _____ each other _____ years. (know)
6. Rosie _____ her friend Scott _____ he joined the ballet. (not see)

5 Make questions. Use the present perfect with *how long*.

1. you / know / Joanna and Faye / ?
   How long have you known Joanna and Faye?
2. you / be / at this drama college / ?
   _____
3. Jack / want / to be an actor / ?
   _____
4. Yasmin / have / this talent / ?
   _____
5. your dad / play / the piano / ?
   _____
6. they / live / in Hollywood / ?
   _____

6 Complete the interview. Use one word in each space.

Sandy
Hi, sorry I'm late. How 1) *long* have you been here?

Interviewer
I 2) _____ only been here for five minutes, don't worry. So, Sandy, 3) _____ long have you been in the group 'The Hot Heads'?

Sandy
4) _____ last July, but I've known the others in the group 5) _____ a long time.

Interviewer
So what made you start your own group?

Sandy
Well, we 6) _____ been interested in music for years and always wanted to play in a band.

Interviewer
Right, and you play lead guitar, Sandy?

Sandy
Yes, I've 7) _____ the guitar since I was about six. My dad taught me how to play.

Interviewer
And you won a national talent competition recently?

Sandy
Yes, that was amazing. We've won three competitions 8) _____ we started the band, but that was the biggest.

Interviewer
Well, I wish you lots of luck for your future music career!

Sandy
Thank you.

LISTENING

1 🔊 **9.1 Listen to Jacob talking to his teacher about a theatre trip. Complete Jacob's notes.**

School theatre trip
1. Teachers on trip: Mrs Hammond and Mr _Green_
2. Name of theatre: .... Theatre
3. Date of trip: .... th June
4. Meet at: ....
5. Cost of trip: £ ....
6. Do not take: .... or phones

2 🔊 **9.2 Listen again and choose the correct answer, A or B.**

1. Has Mrs Hammond been to the Rose Theatre before?
   - (A) no
   - B yes
2. What website has Jacob just been on?
   - A the school website
   - B the theatre website
3. What has the theatre just sent Mrs Hammond?
   - A the times of the visit
   - B tickets for the visit
4. How will they get to the theatre?
   - A on foot
   - B by coach
5. What has Mrs Hammond just written?
   - A a letter to the parents
   - B a letter to the theatre
6. When will Mrs Hammond collect the money for the trip?
   - A the day before the trip
   - B on the day of the trip

GRAMMAR
Present perfect with just

1 Make sentences. Use the present perfect with *just*.

1. Kathy / send / an email to Pete.
   Kathy's just sent an email to Pete.
2. I / start / a great book.
3. They / choose / the winner.
4. The magician / arrive / on stage.
5. Danny / appear / in a new film.
6. She / join / a rock band.

2 Complete the short conversations. Use *just* and the present perfect form of these verbs.

| buy | finish | ~~leave~~ | phone | see | tell |

1. Where's Ben, Mum?
   He's at his music club. He _'s just left_ to catch a bus.
2. What are you laughing at?
   This comedian on TV. He .... the funniest joke!
3. Where are you going?
   To the cinema. Jake .... and he's got some free tickets.
4. What's in that bag?
   New ballet shoes – I .... them. Do you want to have a look?
5. What's the matter, Sophie?
   I wanted to watch my favourite soap opera on TV and it ....
6. Dad, do you know where my new DVD is?
   Yes, it's on the kitchen table, I .... it.

64 GOLD EXPERIENCE

09 Let me entertain you

SPEAKING SKILLS

1 Put the words in the correct order.
1 shall / we / What / ? / watch /
   What shall we watch?
2 love / I / fiction / films / . / science
3 . / watch / Let's / a / comedy
4 I / films / like / really /. / action / don't
5 about / ? / horror / a / film / How /
6 boring / I / . / think / films/ romantic / are

2 Complete the conversation with these words.

Cool   Really   ~~Do~~   shall   How   See   love   let's

Jack: Hi, Alice!
Alice: Hi, Jack. 1) *Do* you want to watch a DVD at my house?
Jack: Yeah, great! What 2) _____ we watch?
Alice: Well, I've got lots of DVDs. I 3) _____ romantic films.
Jack: 4) _____ ? I think they're boring. I love horror films, though!
Alice: Oh, I don't really like scary films. 5) _____ about an action film?
Jack: Yes, 6) _____ watch an action film.
Alice: 7) _____ ! See you at about five?
Jack: Great! 8) _____ you later!

WRITING

1 Put the parts of Matt's email in the correct order.

A Hope you can come! Matt _____
B I'm going camping on the weekend of the first, but I'm free on the eighth. Do you want to go and see Black Boots with me? The tickets aren't very expensive – they're only £10. _____
C Hi, Rob, how's it going? __1__
D The Angels are playing on 1 March and Black Boots are playing on 8 March. _____
E The tickets go on sale next week. My dad's getting me and my brother a ticket. Text me before Monday and he can get you a ticket, too. _____
F Have you seen the advert for the concerts at the town hall? They look brilliant! _____

2 Complete the email with one word for each space.

Hey, Isobel, 1) *how* are things?

What are you doing 2) _____ 7 November? 3) _____ you seen the poster for the music festival at the football stadium? One Life are playing at the festival – they're my favourite band! I've got all their albums, 4) _____ I've never seen them in concert. Do you want to go to the festival 5) _____ me? My mum said I can go for my birthday 6) _____ I can take a friend! I think 7) _____ will be great!

8) _____ me know what you think.

Freya x

3 You have seen an advert for a music and dance festival in your town. The festival is on for three days, but you can only go on one day. Write an email to your friend suggesting you go together.

10 Eat well, feel well

READING

1 Read the article and match these headings with the paragraphs.

> Hold your nose and take a bite!
> Are those pieces of meat in my biscuit?
> ~~Would you like some salt and ketchup on that, madam?~~
> Salty, sweet … and a bit hot?
> A drink and a dessert in one?

Unusual snacks and drinks from around the world

When you need a snack and a drink, what do you usually have? Perhaps a biscuit and a glass of milk? For some people, their choice of snack and drink is a little more unusual!

1) _Would you like some salt and ketchup on that, madam?_
In Fremantle, Australia, people are eating a very unusual kind of ice cream as they walk along the beach. They're eating fish-and-chip-flavoured ice cream! You don't need to ask who thought of this idea: a fish and chip shop owner!

2) _____
In Japan, you can find a drink called Teagurt. Can you guess what it is from its name? It's iced tea with the flavour of peach yoghurt. What does it taste like? It tastes first like tea, then like peach juice, then like yoghurt.

3) _____
Durian is a popular tropical fruit in Indonesia and Malaysia. Why is this fruit an unusual snack? Durian has a smell so strong that you're not allowed to eat it in many hotels and public places. Some people say durian smells like old onions or smelly socks, but for others it's the perfect fruit.

4) _____
The British love crisps and they love unusual flavours. You have probably tried salt and vinegar crisps, cheese and onion flavour or crisps flavoured with paprika. But have you ever tried chilli chocolate flavoured crisps? In the UK this is just one of the strange flavours you can buy.

5) _____
Probably the most unusual cookies in the US are chocolate chip bacon cookies. To make these, you have to cook the bacon first and then add it to the cookie mixture before you put it in the oven. It might sound strange but people love them!

2 Find words in the article that match these meanings.

1 food that you eat between meals: s_nacks_
2 something white you use to add flavour to food: s_____
3 sweet food that you eat at the end of a main meal: d_____
4 exactly right for someone: p_____
5 unusual or odd: s_____
6 the equipment you use to bake food: o_____

VOCABULARY
Food and health

1 Look at the pictures and complete the sentences with the correct form of these verbs.

| ~~bake~~ barbecue boil fry grill roast |

1 Noah _baked_ some bread at school yesterday.

2 Can you _____ some water for the vegetables, please?

3 My dad enjoys _____ in the summer.

4 Mum's in the kitchen at the moment. She _____ a chicken for dinner.

GOLD EXPERIENCE

10 Eat well, feel well

5 We always .... our meat. It's healthier that way.

6 I .... the chicken for the salad this morning.

2 Complete the sentences with adjectives formed from the verbs in brackets.
1 My parents had _grilled_ fish and salad for lunch. (grill)
2 I love the smell of freshly .... bread. (bake)
3 My brother hates .... eggs. (fry)
4 We all love .... food in our family. (barbecue)
5 My grandma always gives us meat and .... vegetables for dinner. (boil)
6 I love my mum's .... potatoes. (roast)

3 Complete the table with these words.

~~chips~~   chocolate   crisps   ice cream   lemon   lime

sweet	salty	sour
	chips	

4 Choose the correct words.
1 I have to do regular _exercise_/_fit_ now I'm in the basketball team.
2 I love _junk food_/_snacks_. My favourite is hamburger and fries.
3 Driving everywhere can be _unfit_/_unhealthy_. It's a good idea to walk more.
4 It's _fit_/_healthy_ to do twenty minutes of exercise three times a week.
5 At school we have fruit for a _snack_/_meal_ at morning break.
6 Sophie is very _fit_/_unhealthy_. She can run up the hill in five minutes!

5 Complete the email with these words.

do   ~~fit~~   healthy   junk   regular   unfit

Hi, Robbie
Do you still go to the gym? I want to get 1) _fit_ because I'd like to join the school volleyball team. I've stopped eating 2) .... food and I eat lots of 3) .... food like fruit and vegetables. I'm not very 4) ...., but it's been a long time since I played any sport. I need to start doing some 5) .... exercise soon. They'll choose the players for the volleyball team next month. What kind of exercise do you 6) ....?
Can you help me?
Thanks.
Jennie

6 Add _i_, _e_, _a_, _o_ or _u_ to make nouns about not feeling well.
1 c_o_ld
2 h___d___ch___
3 s___r___ thr___t
4 c___gh
5 st___m___ch___ch___
6 t___mp___r___t___r___
7 t___th___ch___

7 Choose the correct answer, A, B or C.

1 Are you OK, Jacob? Your eyes and nose are red.
   I've got a _cold_. I feel terrible!
   A toothache (B) cold C stomachache
2 Do you want some of this chocolate cake?
   I can't. I've got really bad _____ and it hurts when I eat.
   A temperature B headache C toothache
3 Why are you wearing that thick scarf, Rosie?
   I've got a _____ and it feels better when my neck's warm.
   A sore throat B temperature C stomachache
4 Have I got a _____ ?
   Yes, it's 39°C. You're very hot. I'll give you some medicine.
   A temperature B toothache C cough
5 Your _____ sounds bad! Do you want a glass of water?
   I'm OK, thanks. It happens every time I speak. I think I need to go to the doctor's.
   A toothache B cough C stomachache
6 Why have you got your eyes closed?
   I've got a bad _____ and the light makes it feel worse.
   A headache B sore throat C cough

8 Complete the email with these words.

> barbecue   exercise   ~~fitter~~   food   fried
> sweet   vegetables

Hi, Yan
We've got a new basketball teacher and he's given us a training programme. He says it will make us 1) _fitter_ and healthier. I hope it makes us win some more basketball matches, too! The training programme tells us how much 2) _____ we need to do every week and also what 3) _____ to eat. I need to eat five types of fruit or 4) _____ a day. I should only grill or 5) _____ meat. I shouldn't eat any 6) _____ food – which means no junk food! I also shouldn't eat too much 7) _____ food, like biscuits. I only started it yesterday so I will tell you how it goes!
Callum

GRAMMAR
Obligation and prohibition

1 Choose the correct words.

1 You *must*/*mustn't* cook chicken well before you eat it.
2 I *must*/*mustn't* check the cake in the oven. I think it's ready now.
3 You *must*/*mustn't* touch the oven. It's very hot.
4 Jo has toothache and *must*/*mustn't* eat any sweets.
5 You *must*/*mustn't* forget to switch the oven off after you use it.
6 The children *must*/*mustn't* wash their hands before dinner.

2 Complete the sentences with *must* or *mustn't*.

1 You _mustn't_ eat food here.

2 You _____ wash your hands.

3 You _____ play ball games here.

4 You _____ be quiet.

5 You _____ use your mobile phone.

6 You _____ bring dogs here.

10 Eat well, feel well

3 Complete the sentences with *must* or *mustn't* and these verbs.

> bring   do   ~~eat~~   keep   remember   see

1 My mum says I _mustn't eat_ sweets before dinner.
2 You _____ the milk in the fridge or it will go bad.
3 Athletes _____ regular exercise.
4 You _____ to drink lots of water when you do exercise.
5 Cara _____ the dentist about her toothache.
6 You _____ any food into the computer room.

4 Look at Joseph's list for his birthday party and complete the sentences with *needs to* and *doesn't need to*.

Party – things to do!	Done
phone DJ	✓
buy cola and juice
get some snacks
invite friends	✓
buy new jeans
borrow party lights from Gavin	✓

1 Joseph _doesn't need to_ phone the DJ.
2 Joseph _____ buy cola and juice.
3 Joseph _____ get some snacks.
4 Joseph _____ invite his friends.
5 Joseph _____ buy new jeans.
6 Joseph _____ borrow party lights from Gavin.

5 Choose the correct words.

1 John *needs/doesn't need* to eat more fruit and vegetables. He doesn't eat enough healthy food.
2 I *don't need/need* a snack. I'm really hungry and I can't wait until dinner.
3 Kelly *doesn't need/needs* to do more exercise. She's very fit and plays lots of sports.
4 We *don't need/need* to fry the onions first. Then we add the chicken and peppers later.
5 You *need/don't need* to wash your hands before you prepare food.
6 You *don't need/need* to buy more juice. We have lots in the fridge.
7 Rob *needs/doesn't need* to go to the doctor's. He feels better now.

LISTENING

1 🔊 10.1 Listen to a telephone conversation between Carla and her friend Leo. Answer the question.

What are Carla and Leo going to cook tomorrow?
_____

2 🔊 10.2 Listen again and choose the correct answer, A, B or C.

1 Which teacher is doing the cookery lesson?
   A Mr Franks   B Mrs Sharp   **C Mr Townsend**
2 When are they going to eat the food?
   A at lunchtime
   B at home after school
   C at the school party
3 What are some of the other students baking?
   A cakes   B bread   C biscuits
4 What should the students bring to the cookery lesson?
   A flour   B vegetables   C cheese
5 Why does Leo think it's better to buy pizzas for the party?
   A Because he's lazy.
   B Because he thinks it's cheaper.
   C Because he thinks his pizza won't taste nice.
6 What should the students do before they leave the cookery lesson?
   A do the washing up
   B write in their school diary
   C put on their coats

GRAMMAR
should

1 Complete the sentences. Use *should* or *shouldn't* and the verbs in brackets.

1. You look hot. You *should have* (have) a cold drink.
2. Mark is very tired. He _____ (get) more sleep.
3. You _____ (ask) Sam to help you with your homework. He's good at maths.
4. Jack _____ (go) swimming today. He's got a bad cold.
5. Alice _____ (enter) a cooking competition. She's really good.
6. My dad _____ (put) so much salt on his food. It's very unhealthy.
7. William and Ben _____ (leave) home earlier. They're always late for school.

2 Choose the best answer, A, B or C.

1. I can't sleep because I've got a big exam tomorrow.
   - **A** You shouldn't worry so much. ✓
   - B You must study more.
   - C You don't have to sleep.
2. Do you want to come to the park with us?
   - A I don't need to go. I'm meeting my mum.
   - B I mustn't leave the park. I'm meeting my mum.
   - C I'm meeting my mum and I mustn't be late.
3. Your cough is getting worse. I'll call the doctor.
   - A Thanks, but you shouldn't. I've got an appointment for this afternoon.
   - B Thanks, but you don't need to. I've got an appointment for this afternoon.
   - C Thanks, but you must. I've got an appointment for this afternoon.
4. Are you ready for school?
   - A Nearly. I just need to brush my teeth.
   - B No, I shouldn't be ready in five minutes.
   - C I mustn't be late for school.
5. Can I borrow your sports bag, Dan?
   - A Yes, you should.
   - B OK, but you must give it back to me.
   - C You don't need to borrow it.
6. I want to get fit. What should I do?
   - A You shouldn't do regular exercise.
   - B You mustn't do regular exercise.
   - C You need to do regular exercise.

3 Complete the text with the best answer, A, B or C, for each space.

Recipe for a great party!

- You 1) *need* to invite a good group of friends. You can't have a good party without a good group of people.
- Be careful how you invite your friends. You 2) _____ tell people about your party on a social networking site. You don't want hundreds of people to arrive at your party!
- You 3) _____ make sure that everyone has enough to eat and drink.
- Good music is very important. You 4) _____ to get a DJ, but you 5) _____ have a good variety of music to play.
- Lastly, you 6) _____ forget to take some photos — they're a great way to remember the party!

1	A must	B should	**C need** ✓
2	A shouldn't	B must	C don't need
3	A mustn't	B should	C need
4	A don't need	B shouldn't	C mustn't
5	A need	B must	C shouldn't
6	A mustn't	B don't need	C should

10 Eat well, feel well

SPEAKING SKILLS

1 Match (1–6) with (A–F) to make sentences.

1 What's the C
2 What's ___
3 Are you feeling ___
4 I've got a ___
5 You should ___
6 You shouldn't eat ___

A stomachache.
B go to bed.
C matter?
D wrong?
E so many sweets.
F all right?

2 Choose the correct words to complete the conversations.

1 **A** Are you OK?
   B I've got a headache and *a/some/the* temperature.
   A You *are/shouldn't/don't* go to school today.

2 **A** What's *a/the/your* matter?
   B I've got toothache.
   A You should see the *doctor/vet/dentist*.

3 **A** What *are/be/'s* wrong?
   B I've got a *sore/cough/hard* throat.
   A You should drink some warm honey and lemon.

WRITING

1 Put the words in the correct order.

1 not / ? / try / learning / Why / a new sport
   Why not try learning a new sport?

2 to / important / lots of water / . / It's / drink

3 It's / eat / too much sugar / not to / . / important

4 cycle to school / a good idea / . / It's / to

5 fried food every day / eat / . / not a good idea / It's / to /

6 should / You / more time / spend / . / in the fresh air

2 Complete the letters with these words.

> ~~but~~   try   should   not   important
> idea   shouldn't   because

Hi,
I'm fifteen years old and I can't get to sleep. I feel tired, 1) *but* when I go to bed I can't fall asleep. It's really annoying 2) _____ I'm always tired the next day. What can I do?
Georgia

Dear Georgia,
You're not alone! Lots of people have problems getting to sleep sometimes. There are some things you can do to help yourself. For example, it's 3) _____ not to spend a lot of time on the computer before you go to bed. It's a good 4) _____ to have a bath or a warm drink of milk before bedtime. These can help you relax. Why not 5) _____ doing some exercise after school or go for a walk outside? Exercise and fresh air can help you sleep. The most important thing is 6) _____ to worry about it. When you can't sleep, you 7) _____ lie in bed and worry. You 8) _____ do something like read a book until you feel tired again.
Good luck!
Rosie

3 Kate wants to get fit, but doesn't want to spend any money. Write a letter of advice to her for an online advice page.

Revision Units 9 – 10

VOCABULARY

1 Complete the conversations with these words.

> chat show   documentary
> ~~horror film~~   romantic films
> soap opera   sports programme

1. I really want to watch this _horror film_ – I love scary films.
   Me too, but you need to be 18 to watch that film.
2. I love that new singer, Rocco. Have you heard him?
   Yes, he's great. There's an interview with him on a _____ tonight.
3. Have you heard of this _____? It's called 'Hollywood Lights'.
   Yes, it's great. It's about two rich families who are always fighting with each other.
4. Did you watch the football match this afternoon?
   No, I didn't. I'm going to watch some of it on the _____ later.
5. What's your sister watching?
   It's a boring film about two people who fall in love. I hate _____!
6. You should do your homework now, Luke.
   I am, Mum. I'm watching this _____ about mountains for geography.

2 Choose the correct words.

1. We're going to *bake*/*boil* some cakes at school tomorrow.
2. One of the healthiest ways to cook meat is to *fry*/*grill* it.
3. Have you ever *barbecued*/*baked* fish on a wood fire? It's really nice.
4. I love the smell of *roast*/*boiled* chicken when it comes out of the oven.
5. Can you *boil*/*fry* some water for the potatoes, please?
6. I've got some oil left in the pan. Would you like a *boiled*/*fried* egg?

3 Complete the review of a TV programme with these words.

> audience   comedian   contestants   funny
> judges   show   ~~talent show~~   TV

The Great Cooking Contest

I love *The Great Cooking Contest*. It's like a 1) _talent show_ for teenage cooks. There are ten 2) _____ and every week they have to cook different things. They do the cooking in a TV studio in front of an 3) _____. At the end of the 4) _____ they get marks for their cooking. There are four 5) _____ who give marks. Three of them are famous chefs, but one judge is a 6) _____. She's really 7) _____. I think this is the best programme on 8) _____!

4 Choose the correct words.

Alex: Hi, Harriet. Do you do 1) *fit*/*regular* exercise?
Harriet: Yes, I go to the gym every week and play basketball on Tuesdays. Why?
Alex: I'm really 2) *unfit*/*junk*, but I don't know what to do.
Harriet: Why don't you join my gym? It's good fun. You also need to stop eating 3) *healthy*/*junk* food like that burger you're eating now!
Alex: I know, but I love 4) *grilled*/*fried* food!
Harriet: Well, you can still eat it sometimes, but you need to eat more 5) *healthy*/*boiled* food.
Alex: Yes, you're right. Can I come with you next time you go to the gym? I haven't done any 6) *snacks*/*exercise* for ages, so can you show me what to do?
Harriet: Yes, sure. I'll send you a text.
Alex: Thanks.

REVISION Units 9 – 10

GRAMMAR

1 Complete these conversations with *just* and the present perfect form of the verbs in brackets.

1. What's the matter, Emily?
   I **'ve just bitten** (bite) into this orange and it's really sour!
2. Why isn't Danny eating any ice cream?
   He _____ (come) back from the dentist and he's got toothache.
3. Something smells really nice. What is it?
   My dad _____ (bake) some bread. We can have some for lunch.
4. I'm really hungry. Is there anything to eat?
   I _____ (grill) some sausages. Do you want some in a sandwich?
5. Rebecca and Joe don't look very well. Are they all right?
   They _____ (eat) two big pizzas and I think they've got stomachache.
6. Do you want an orange juice?
   No, thanks – I _____ (drink) a bottle of cola.

2 Choose the correct words.

> **Talent Show**
> Saturday 12 March
> (13-17 yrs only)

1. All talent show contestants *must*/*mustn't* be between 13 and 17 years old.

> **White chocolate biscuits**
> Baking time: 10 minutes at 180°C

2. You *don't need to*/*need to* bake these biscuits at 180°C.

> Do not take more than 8 in 24 hours.

3. You *should*/*mustn't* have more than eight sore throat sweets in a day.

> **Mayflower Singing Club**
> – all levels welcome!

4. You *need*/*don't need* to be a really good singer to join the singing club.

> **Adults:** 6 g of salt or less a day

5. Adults *must*/*shouldn't* eat more than 6 g of salt a day.

> Please switch off your mobile phone.

6. The audience *must*/*don't need to* switch off their mobile phones during the show.

3 Complete the sentences with *for* or *since*.

1. I haven't eaten chocolate cake **since** my birthday last year.
2. My brother's really fit. He's been in our school football team _____ three years.
3. I've had a headache _____ I woke up this morning.
4. This actor hasn't been in a film _____ 2012.
5. I haven't watched this soap opera _____ ages.
6. I haven't bought any junk food _____ the last two months. I'm trying to be healthy.
7. Tom's had a bad cough _____ Friday. I think he should see the doctor.
8. You only need to fry this fish _____ five minutes.

4 Complete these questions and answers with one word in each space.

1. How long have you been a magician?
   Since I was 13 years old.
2. Should I roast the vegetables at 180°C?
   No, the oven needs _____ be hotter than that.
3. When will dinner be ready?
   About 1 o'clock. I _____ just put the chicken in the oven.
4. What do I _____ to do to enter the talent show?
   You must fill in this form.
5. Is this your first performance?
   No, I've been an actor _____ years.
6. _____ we need to sing and dance in the show?
   Yes, you do. Can you dance?

11 More than a job

READING

1 Read the article and choose the correct answer, A, B, C or D.

Could you work with your mum or dad?

We visited four teenagers who help their parents in the family business to find out what they think.

When Sam Jenkins isn't at school, he helps his mum at her café, Cornerstone. So, does Sam mind working in the family business in his free time? 'I really enjoy it. I started working here when I was twelve. I know most of the customers and so it's a very friendly atmosphere.' Sam usually works as a waiter, but if it's very busy, he sometimes helps the chef. Sam thinks it's a good thing for teenagers to work with their parents. 'If kids work with their parents, they can learn about the business world and learn useful skills.'

James and Kirsty are twins and their parents own the Maple Hotel. James and Kirsty help their mum and dad in lots of ways. They help prepare the dining room for the hotel guests, clean the rooms and work on the reception desk. Of course, they also go to school and so they only help if they have time. Kirsty says she enjoys helping in the summer the most. 'It's busier and more tiring, but it's always fun.' Would they like to own their own hotel? Kirsty's not sure, but James answers with a strong 'No!' He's more interested in working with computers.

Emilia works at her dad's garage. Most of the time her job is to make the tea and answer the phone. Emilia would like to be a mechanic when she's older. If it's not very busy, her dad teaches her about cars. 'Dad has taught me a lot about being a mechanic and working in a garage. It's always fun with Dad because he's not really like my boss.' Does Emilia think there is anything bad about working in the family business? 'Sometimes it's hard when all my friends are going out and I have to help at the garage. Most of the time, though, I love it!'

1 Which person says when they started helping in the family business?
 A Emilia B James C Kirsty D <u>Sam</u>
2 Which person says they want to do the same job as their parent?
 A Emilia B James C Kirsty D Sam
3 Which person says they sometimes work in a kitchen?
 A Emilia B James C Kirsty D Sam
4 Which person says they would like to work with technology?
 A Emilia B James C Kirsty D Sam
5 Which person says which season they prefer to work in?
 A Emilia B James C Kirsty D Sam
6 Which person says they sometimes miss going out with their friends?
 A Emilia B James C Kirsty D Sam

2 Find words in the article that match these meanings.
1 the feeling in a place: a *tmosphere*
2 a man who brings food or drinks to customers: w_____
3 get something ready: p_____
4 the people who are staying at a hotel: g_____
5 pick up a phone when it rings: a_____
6 difficult: h_____

11 More than a job

VOCABULARY
The world of work

1 Match the words (1–6) with (a–f) to make jobs.

1 bus — b
2 football — d
3 maths — f
4 pop — e
5 police — c
6 shop — a

a assistant
b driver
c officer
d player
e singer
f teacher

2 Choose the correct words.

1 Freya wants to be a *police officer*/*shop assistant*. She wants to make her city a safe place.
2 Kiera's dad was a *pop singer*/*football player* when he was young. He was very famous and won lots of matches with his team.
3 Dan's mum is a *shop assistant*/*bus driver*. She takes people around the city centre.
4 My cousin is studying at university. He wants to be a *pop singer*/*maths teacher* and work with small children.
5 Liam's dad is a *shop assistant*/*police officer* in the city centre. He works in a department store.
6 My parents are both English teachers, but I want to be a *maths teacher*/*pop singer*. I love music and I'd like to be famous one day.

3 Complete the sentences with these jobs.

doctor   journalist   mechanic
~~police officer~~   receptionist   waitress

1 My cousin's a *police officer*. He works at the large police station in the city centre.
2 Shane's a .... for the *Evening Star* newspaper, but he spends half his time at a desk in the office.
3 Maria's a .... at the new Italian restaurant in town.
4 Rafaela is a .... at the City Plaza hotel. Her job is to help the hotel guests and answer the telephone.
5 I'm a .... and I fix cars in a garage with my dad and brother.
6 Lauren's a .... in the city hospital. She helps old people who are ill.

4 Match these places with the pictures.

garage   hospital   hotel   ~~office~~
police station   restaurant

1 *office*

2 ....
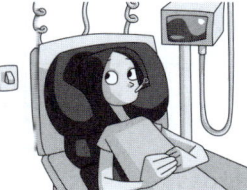

3 ....

4 ....

5 ....

6 ....
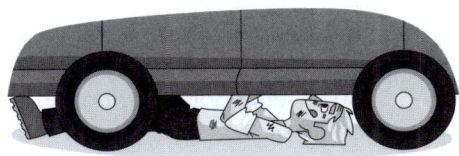

5 Complete the crossword.

Across
2 people who play music on the radio or at discos
3 someone whose job is to paint things such as walls or doors
4 someone who does paintings or drawings
6 someone who cleans houses, offices or other public places

Down
1 a woman who works in business
5 someone who cooks for people in a restaurant

6 Complete the sentences with these words.

chef   ~~garage~~   hospital   journalist   office   receptionist

1 Where's Mum's car?
   It's in the _garage_. It's got a problem with the engine.
2 Is your brother a waiter in a restaurant?
   No, he's the _____. He makes the food.
3 Where's Dad?
   He's talking to the hotel _____. He wants to change our room.
4 I didn't know Sam worked in a _____.
   Yes, he's a doctor.
5 What job do you want when you're older?
   I don't know, but something outside. I couldn't work in an _____ all day.
6 You're very good at writing stories, Amy. You should be a _____.
   Do you think so? I'd love to work for a newspaper.

7 Match the sentence beginnings (1–6) with the endings (A–F).

1 Martin's uncle is the _D_
2 Lucy enjoys being part of _____
3 A good way to earn _____
4 I've got time _____
5 Georgina and Tom work _____
6 Isobel wants to get a _____

A money is to get a summer job.
B good job when she finishes university.
C hard in the restaurant, but they enjoy it.
D boss of the company.
E off today because I worked all weekend.
F a team in her new job.

8 Choose the correct words.

Hi, Jason

I've found a great 1) *job/work* for the summer. I'm going to be a 2) *waitress/waiter* in a beach café! It's my aunt's café, so I hope she won't make me work too 3) *hard/difficult*! I'll be 4) *piece/part* of a team of five waiters and we're all the same age, so I think it will be lots of fun. I won't 5) *do/earn* lots of money, but I will be next to the beach all summer. We'll get an hour 6) *off/over* for lunch so I plan to go swimming every day.

Anyway, how about you? Have you got a 7) *good/well* job for the summer?

Simon

11 More than a job

GRAMMAR
Zero conditional

1 Match the sentence beginnings (1–6) with the endings (A–F).

1 The chef is happy _B_
2 If I work Saturday and Sunday, ___
3 If the shop is very busy, ___
4 My boss is always unhappy ___
5 If I feel very ill, ___
6 Teachers are pleased ___

A the shop assistants work more hours.
B if everyone in the restaurant enjoys their food.
C I go to the doctor.
D if all their students do their homework.
E if anyone arrives at work late.
F I always get Monday off.

2 Complete the zero conditional sentences. Use the correct form of the verbs in brackets.

1 We __work__ (work) quietly if the boss __is__ (be) in the office.
2 Rachel ___ (get) extra money if she ___ (sell) a lot of clothes.
3 If he ___ (have) time off, Jacob ___ (like) to go surfing.
4 I always ___ (feel) nervous if I ___ (have) an exam.
5 If it ___ (rain), we ___ (work) inside.
6 Sean ___ (earn) more money if he ___ (work) on Sundays.

First conditional

3 Put the words in the correct order to make sentences.

1 he'll pass / If / his exams / hard, / he studies / .
   If he studies hard, he'll pass his exams.
2 a mechanic / at his dad's garage / he becomes / if / Simon will work / .
3 angry / we don't finish / Our boss will be / our work / if / .
4 she'll be / a job at the hospital, / Danielle gets / If / part of a big team / .
5 if / a famous pop singer / a lot of records / Grace will be / she sells / .
6 you want / you'll have to / to leave work early, / If / ask the boss / .

4 Choose the correct words.

1 If I _have_/'ll have time, I'll go swimming after work.
2 William won't be late if he 'll leave/_leaves_ now.
3 If Gabrielle works/will work hard, she will earn more money.
4 Mark's boss will be angry if he 's/will be late again.
5 If I earn enough money, I buy/'ll buy some new trainers.
6 The party is/will be inside if the weather is bad.

5 Complete the first conditional sentences. Use the correct form of the verbs in brackets.

1 If we __go__ (go) now, we __'ll get__ (get) to the restaurant on time.
2 They ___ (put) the tables outside the café if it ___ (be) sunny.
3 You ___ (be) hungry at work if you ___ (not have) some food now.
4 My boss ___ (phone) me if I ___ (need) to work tomorrow.
5 If you ___ (like) working in a team, you ___ (love) the job at the fairground.
6 If I ___ (get) this job, I ___ (be) really happy.

LISTENING

1 🔊 **11.1** Mark's school wants parents to come into the classroom and talk about their jobs. Listen to Mark telling his dad what jobs some of the parents do. Choose the jobs you hear.

1 chef
2 nurse
3 <u>police officer</u>
4 teacher
5 mechanic
6 receptionist
7 businessman
8 doctor
9 taxi driver

2 🔊 **11.2** Listen again and match the people (1–5) with the jobs (a–e).

1 Joe's dad   a police officer
2 Charlotte's mum   b doctor
3 Isobel's dad   c receptionist
4 Harry's mum   d mechanic
5 Tom's mum   e teacher

GRAMMAR
Conditional with *could*

1 Make conditional sentences with *could*.

1 you / like / helping people → you / work in a hospital
   If you like helping people, you could work in a hospital.

2 she / study / hard → go / to university

3 you / like / cooking → be / a chef

4 he / enjoy / working with cars → be / a mechanic

5 Andrea / sing / well → win / the competition

6 Dan / work / hard → get / a better job

2 Complete the conditional sentences. Use the correct form of the verbs in brackets.

Ways to work or study better

Make sure you take regular breaks and get some fresh air. If you 1) ___*feel*___ (feel) tired, you 2) _____ (not work) as well. Also, if you 3) _____ (not drink) enough, you 4) _____ (have) less energy. It's a good idea to have a bottle of water on your desk.

Are you sitting at a tidy desk? If your desk 5) _____ (be) untidy, you 6) _____ (lose) things. Also, think about what you want to do each day. If you 7) _____ (make) a list, you 8) _____ (remember) what you need to do.

3 Complete the text with these words.

> babysit   earn   have to   if   'll   won't   will

Hi, Matt,

I need your help – I'm confused! I want a part-time job, but I don't know which one to choose.
My neighbour has asked me to do some babysitting. 1) ___*If*___ I babysit in the evenings, the children 2) _____ be asleep, so it could be an easy job. I'll 3) _____ money for watching TV! If I 4) _____ at the weekends, though, I 5) _____ see my friends.

The other job is delivering newspapers. If I get this job, I'll 6) _____ get up early. I'll have to deliver the papers before 8 a.m.! But if I take this job, I 7) _____ be free all weekend.

Which job do you think I should take?

Brett

11 More than a job

SPEAKING SKILLS

1 Put the words in the correct order.
1 don't / ? / you/ a / Why / get / job /
   Why don't you get a job?
2 in / about / ? / working / What / café / a
3 could / a / help / in / shop / . / You
4 's / a / . / That / idea / great
5 not / 'm / about / sure / that / . / I
6 not / on / keen / that / I / idea / . / 'm

2 Complete the conversation with these words.

~~but~~   sure   's   could   get   about

Oliver: I usually go to summer camp in the school holidays, 1) *but* I'd love to do something different this year.
Amelia: Why don't you 2) .... a job? You 3) .... do some babysitting for your neighbours, like me.
Oliver: Mmm ... I'm not 4) .... about that.
Amelia: What 5) .... helping out in a café? Lots of the cafés by the beach need extra help in the summer.
Oliver: That 6) .... a good idea – thanks!

WRITING

1 Choose the correct words.
1 Sophie loves helping people. She wants to be a doctor *or/but* a nurse.
2 Jon is a chef. He enjoys his job, *or/but* he doesn't like working every weekend.
3 My mum's a teacher. *However/Or*, she wanted to be an actress when she was younger.
4 *However/Although* Peter enjoys working in the café, he'd like to go to university one day.
5 Once Lisa wanted to be a journalist, *but/or* now she'd like to be a police officer.
6 Charlie would like to be a bus driver *although/or* a taxi driver.

2 Match (1–6) with (a–f) to make sentences.
1 You can find job adverts *d*
2 If you like working outside, ...
3 The best month to look for work ....
4 If you buy a local newspaper, ...
5 I think you could ....
6 If you work at a summer camp, ...

a is May or June.
b teach football to children.
c you could work at the surfing club.
d on the Internet.
e you'll make lots of friends.
f it will have job adverts in it.

3 A friend is moving to your town and wants to find a summer job. Write an email saying what summer jobs your friend could do and explaining the best way to find a job.

12 Summer fun!

READING

1 Read the article and choose right (R), wrong (W) or doesn't say (DS) for each sentence.

When bad luck changes to good luck

It's the summer holidays and it's a time for having fun. Maybe you're going on holiday to the beach or spending time at home with friends. Sometimes, though, things can go wrong. Read about three bad experiences that all had unexpected happy endings.

A five-star holiday
Last August we went on holiday to Dublin in Ireland. It was late when we arrived and we were all looking forward to relaxing in our hotel. It was a small, simple hotel outside the city. When we got to the reception desk, the manager told us there were no rooms booked for us. It was a big mistake. The manager was very sorry and offered us rooms in one of their other hotels. We weren't happy, but we agreed to change hotel. When we got to the other hotel, we couldn't believe our eyes! It was a five-star hotel in the city centre. What a lucky mistake!
Jacob, 15

I love my new clothes!
I went to Spain this summer with my grandparents. We travelled by plane to Barcelona. When we arrived at the airport, we went to collect our luggage. We got my grandparents' suitcases, but mine never arrived. The man at the airport took our name and telephone number. Three days later we got a phone call from the airport. They said sorry for losing my suitcase and gave me some money to buy new clothes. I loved shopping in Barcelona and I bought some amazing clothes. I was pleased they lost my suitcase!
Di, 14

The day I met a pop star
Last summer I went to a concert in the park with my two older cousins. My favourite singer, Marc Martin, was performing. Marc was brilliant and sang all our favourite songs. Then, suddenly, I remember feeling very strange, and the next thing I remember, I was lying on the floor! Some people carried me to the back of the stage. They said I was very hot and gave me some water. I felt fine, but was sad that I missed the rest of the concert. Then the most amazing thing happened: Marc Martin came to see if I was OK! My cousins took a photo of me with him. I still have it on my wall at home.
Megan, 15

1 Jacob arrived in Dublin in the morning. _W_
2 Jacob and his family were unhappy when they left the first hotel. ____
3 Di lives with her grandparents. ____
4 The people at the airport found Di's suitcase. ____
5 Megan is younger than her cousins. ____
6 Megan felt very ill when she met Marc Martin. ____

2 Read the article again and choose the correct answer, A or B.

1 Who offered Jacob and his family a different hotel?
   (A) the manager   **B** the receptionist
2 Where was the five-star hotel that Jacob stayed at?
   A next to the first hotel   **B** in the city centre
3 When did Sarah get a phone call from the airport?
   A a week later   **B** a few days later
4 How did Sarah feel about losing her suitcase?
   A happy   **B** sad
5 How did Megan get to the back of the stage?
   A some people helped her
   B she walked by herself
6 What does Megan have on her wall at home?
   A her concert ticket   **B** a picture of her with Marc

VOCABULARY
Holiday words

1 Find and write six things that you could take on holiday with you.

s	f	l	a	p	f	l	o	p	s
u	l	r	u	c	k	s	a	c	k
m	i	v	y	n	e	u	k	l	a
a	p	g	l	a	s	n	u	f	s
c	f	u	m	a	r	g	o	l	e
a	l	a	r	m	c	l	o	c	k
f	o	l	p	h	s	a	l	e	a
l	p	i	t	u	s	s	o	c	n
i	s	p	e	r	d	s	e	d	o
d	s	u	n	c	r	e	a	m	a
t	i	n	t	n	u	s	l	a	r

1 _alarm clock_   4 _____
2 _____   5 _____
3 _____   6 _____

12 Summer fun!

2 Choose the correct words.

1. Where's your *sun cream/alarm clock*? We need to wake up early in the morning.
2. I can't put anything else in my *rucksack/tent*. It's too heavy and it's hurting my back.
3. You're very red. Did you forget to put *flip-flops/sun cream* on?
4. Why are you wearing *sunglasses/an alarm clock*? We're inside a café!
5. There's a hole in my *tent/rucksack*. The rain is coming inside. I can feel it on my head.
6. These *flip-flops/tents* are really old. I can't walk very well in them.

3 Complete the sentences with these words.

> campsite ~~festival~~ map passport
> picnic suitcase

1. There's a great music _festival_ in my city every June.
2. You'll need to show your _____ at the airport.
3. Is this your _____ ? It's very heavy! What's inside it?
4. It's a big _____ with space for 200 tents.
5. Here is our hotel on the _____ . It's that black square next to the road.
6. It's a great day for a _____ . Let's have lunch on the beach.

4 Complete the table with these words and phrases.

> ~~an accident~~ at a friend's house camping fun
> on a campsite on holiday

have	_an accident_
go	
stay	

5 Choose the correct answer, A, B or C.

1. Did you __have__ a good holiday, Tim?
   A stay **B have** C go
2. Paul and Jack aren't here. They _____ to the beach.
   A 've stayed B 've had C 've gone
3. Are you _____ in the same hotel as us?
   A staying B going C having
4. Would you like to _____ a picnic with us?
   A go B stay C have
5. We _____ to an amazing kite festival in Germany.
   A had B went C stayed
6. Thank you for showing us round the city. We _____ a great time!
   A 've stayed B 've gone C 've had
7. We _____ in the same apartment on the beach every year.
   A stay B have C go
8. This is the fifth barbecue we _____ since we arrived!
   A 've stayed B 've had C 've gone

6 Complete the conversation with the correct form of *have*, *go* or *stay*.

Ben: Hi, Rosie. How are you?
Rosie: Hi, Ben. Great, thanks. I've just come back from holiday.
Ben: Really? Where did you go?
Rosie: France. We 1) _went_ on holiday there for two weeks. We 2) _____ a great time.
Ben: Did you go camping?
Rosie: No, we 3) _____ in a really nice apartment. My bedroom had views of the sea. It was fantastic!
Ben: So what did you do there?
Rosie: Well, we 4) _____ to the beach for a swim nearly every day.
Ben: Did you go with your parents?
Rosie: Yes, but we met a really nice family and one evening we all 5) _____ a barbecue on the beach – it was really cool. Did you have a good holiday?
Ben: Yes, thanks.
Rosie: Did you 6) _____ in your uncle's hotel again?
Ben: Yes and we 7) _____ to a kite festival – some of the kites were amazing. I'll show you my photos next time I see you.

Phrasal verbs

7 Complete the conversations with the correct form of these phrasal verbs.

> look for   look out   ~~put on~~
> take off   turn off   turn on

1. It's so sunny I can't read the map.
   Here you are, you can _put on_ my sunglasses.
2. Joe, please _____ your boots before you come in the tent!
   OK, no problem. Shall I leave them here?
3. Can you _____ the radio? I want to listen to the weather forecast.
   Yeah. If it's going to be hot, I'll go for a swim later.
4. What _____ you _____?
   The keys to our hotel room. They're in the rucksack somewhere.
5. _____! Your football nearly hit the barbecue!
   Sorry, Dad, we'll play over there.
6. _____ you _____ your mobile phone?
   Yes, I did it as soon as we got on the plane.

8 Choose the correct words.

Welcome to
Sunnyside Holiday Apartment
Information for guests

You can 1) <u>turn on</u>/look out the air conditioning with the red button near the fridge. Please remember to turn the air conditioning 2) out/off before you leave the apartment.

In the lounge, there is information about local beaches and festivals you can 3) stay/go to.

Can we please ask you to 4) put off/take off dirty shoes before you come in the apartment.

You can 5) have/go a barbecue in the garden. You can find everything you need in the kitchen cupboard.

We hope you will 6) stay/have a great holiday and enjoy our apartment.

GRAMMAR
–ing forms and to infinitive

1 Complete the table with these words and phrases.

> ~~agree~~   bored with   decide   enjoy   forget
> good at   look forward to   want

Followed by	
-ing forms	*to* infinitive
	agree
continue	
	help
interested in	try

2 Match the sentence beginnings (1–6) with the endings (A–F).

1. I love Spain. I'm looking forward to _C_
2. My aunt likes expensive hotels. She isn't interested in __
3. Would you like __
4. I forgot __
5. I love surfing, but my brother doesn't enjoy __
6. Finlay hopes __

A to take my sunglasses on holiday.
B to go to a festival with his friends after their exams.
C visiting Madrid in June.
D doing water sports.
E to go to Brazil next summer?
F going camping with us.

3 Choose the correct words.

1. I'm not interested in <u>taking</u>/to take any photos.
2. Rose and James are looking forward to seeing/see their grandparents.
3. Rachel hopes going/to go to Italy next year.
4. Harvey's bored with swimming/to swim every day.
5. I'd like buying/to buy some new sunglasses for my holiday.
6. Annabel forgot bringing/to bring her flip-flops.

12 Summer fun!

LISTENING

1 🔊 **12.1 Listen to Joshua talking to Zoe about a festival. What kind of festival are they talking about? Choose the correct answer.**

1 a music festival
2 a food festival
3 a balloon festival
4 a kite festival
5 a dance festival

2 🔊 **12.2 Listen again and choose the correct answer, A, B or C.**

1 Who has been to the festival before?
 A only Joshua
 (B) only Zoe
 C Joshua and Zoe
2 How far is the festival from Bristol city centre?
 A about two miles
 B about one mile
 C about three miles
3 How much do tickets to the festival cost?
 A £7
 B £17
 C Nothing – they're free.
4 What bus goes from Bristol bus station to the festival?
 A 388
 B 358
 C 348
5 Which day is Joshua going to the festival?
 A Sunday
 B Friday
 C Saturday
6 What happened to the kite Zoe made at the festival?
 A It's stuck in a tree.
 B It broke at the festival.
 C She left it on the bus.

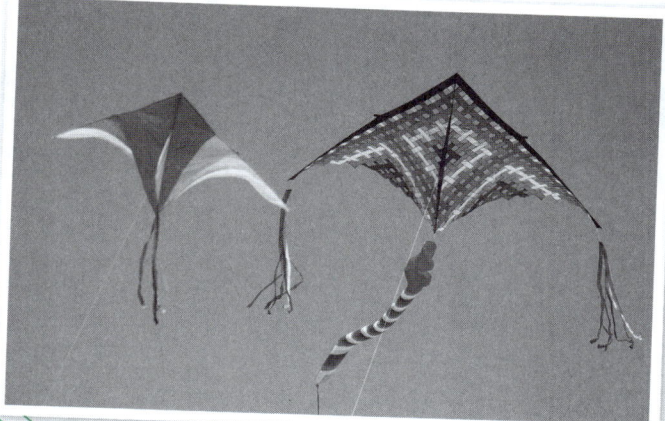

GRAMMAR
Present simple passive

1 Put the words in the correct order to make sentences.

1 is / in the price of the ticket / Transport / included / .
 Transport is included in the price of the ticket.
2 checked / Your bags / at the airport / are / .
3 emailed / is / Information about the apartment / to you / .
4 are / on the beach / Ice creams and cold drinks / sold / .
5 is / on your train ticket / Your seat number / printed / .
6 are / a map of the campsite when you arrive / given / You / .

2 Complete these sentences with *is* or *are*.

1 These bags *are* made by local people.
2 The food _____ cooked in front of you.
3 A free drink _____ given to every hotel guest.
4 Tickets for the festival _____ sold online and in music shops.
5 The campsite _____ used by people of all ages.
6 The boat trips _____ organised by the holiday company.

3 Complete the sentences. Use the present simple passive form of the verbs in brackets.

1. The tourists _are shown_ (show) round the castle by a guide.
2. Dogs _____ (not allow) on the beach.
3. The holiday apartment _____ (advertise) on a holiday website.
4. Breakfast _____ (not include) in the price of the room.
5. Drinks and snacks _____ (sell) at the festival.
6. Our apartment _____ (clean) every day.

4 Complete the text with the correct answer, A, B or C, in each space.

Hi, Tom

Only three weeks to our holiday! I'm really looking forward to 1) _going_ camping. My mum's paid for the campsite. The woman at the campsite says all the information 2) ___ sent by post a week before. I've decided 3) ___ ask for a new tent for my birthday. I'm not interested in 4) ___ a really expensive one, but our family tent is so big and heavy! I've seen a great one in the shops. It's not very expensive and a rucksack is 5) ___ away free with the tent. Do you want to go shopping on Saturday? I'd 6) ___ to get some new trainers before the holiday. Don't forget to 7) ___ your surfboard – there's a great beach near the campsite.

I hope to 8) ___ you on Saturday!

Jenny

	A	B	C
1	go	**(B)** going	gone
2	is	are	be
3	on	to	in
4	got	get	getting
5	given	gives	giving
6	liked	liking	like
7	bring	brought	bringing
8	saw	see	seeing

5 Complete the postcard with one word in each space.

Dear Sam

Spain is great! The apartment we're staying in is really cool and we 1) _'re_ allowed to use the swimming pool at the hotel next door. I'm quite good 2) _____ speaking Spanish now and I've made some friends here. I'm going to a beach party tomorrow – I can't wait! I bought a really nice necklace today. It 3) _____ made of shells. I'm going to wear it to the beach party. The town where we're staying also has a music and dance festival this weekend. The whole town 4) _____ decorated with lights and looks really pretty at night. I'm really looking forward to 5) _____ to the festival. I hope 6) _____ go with my new friends José and Cristina.

Love

Julie

12 Summer fun!

SPEAKING SKILLS

1 Choose the correct answer.
1. Where *is/does* it?
2. When is *them/it* open?
3. *When/What* can you do there?
4. How *much/many* does it cost?
5. How do you *getting/get* there?
6. How much is it *for/of* under eighteens?

2 Read the conversation. Choose which sentence fits each space.

> Cool. I'd like to go there!   When is it open?
> ~~That sounds good. Where is it?~~
> And what can you do there?   How much is it?

Emily: I'm going to a summer camp this year.
Theo: 1) *That sounds good. Where is it?*
Emily: It's at Sandy Beach. It's great there.
Theo: 2) _____
Emily: It's open from 18 July to 29 August.
Theo: 3) _____
Emily: It's really cheap – only £6 per day.
Theo: 4) _____
Emily: Oh, there are lots to of things to do. You can go swimming, sailing or surfing, and there's a DJ every evening in the club house.
Theo: 5) _____

WRITING

1 Put the words in the correct order.
1. brilliant / there's / because / lots / do / . / It's / to
   It's brilliant because there's lots to do.
2. going / . / there / lots of / because / you / I / see / enjoy / animals
   _____
3. really / . / because / go / It's / you / cool / can / climbing / rock
   _____
4. because / great / all / open / year / . / It's / it's
   _____
5. love / to / going / it's / the water park / We / because / fun / good / .
   _____
6. about / you / really / interesting / . / learn / because / history / It's
   _____

2 Complete the blog with these phrases.

> the Kowmung Music Festival
> have a picnic
> ~~you can swim in the lots of different pools~~
> without going to the beach
> it shows you how people lived a long time ago
> there are lots of activities to do, like rock climbing and cycling

Great_days_out_blog.com

Aqualand
I love water parks and my favourite day trip is to Aqualand in Saint-Cyr-sur-Mer. I enjoy going there because 1) *you can swim in the lots of different pools*. It's a great way to spend a hot summer's day 2) _____. The park is open from June to September.
Frederic, 15, France

Blue Mountains
I love doing things outdoors and I often go the Blue Mountains in Australia. It's great because 3) _____. There are also lots of different events each year. For example, 4) _____.
Grace, 14, Australia

Warwick Castle
Warwick Castle in England is really interesting. It's really old. Some of the castle was built in 914! It's really cool because 5) _____. There are some really good ghost stories! It's amazing to walk round and you can 6) _____ in the castle gardens. The castle is open all year.
Martin, 15, England

3 Write a blog about the best place for tourists to visit in your town or city. Include the name of the place, where it is, what you can do there and why it is interesting. Remember to add any important information for visitors.

Revision Units 11 – 12

VOCABULARY

1 Choose the correct words.

1. You need to *turn on*/*put on* your uniform before you start work – you can't wear your own clothes.
2. Can you *put on*/*turn off* the lights when you leave the office, please?
3. Where's the best place to *look for*/*look out* a part-time job?
4. You need to *turn off*/*take off* any jewellery you're wearing when you work in the kitchen.
5. *Look for*/*Look out*! You nearly dropped all the glasses.
6. Can you *turn on*/*take off* the radio, please? I always like to listen to music while I'm working.

2 Match the sentences (1–6) with the sentences (A–F).

1. Mark is the hotel receptionist. C
2. Jenny is a journalist. ___
3. Kerry is a mechanic. ___
4. Lucas is a DJ. ___
5. Lisa is a doctor. ___
6. Ben is a chef. ___

A He cooks in a five-star restaurant in Paris.
B She fixes cars and motorbikes.
C He answers the phone and talks to guests.
D She writes in a famous newspaper.
E People pay him to play music at parties.
F She works in a hospital in Sydney.

3 Choose the correct answer, A, B or C.

1. My dad's a painter. Last week he __had__ an accident and fell off his ladder, but he's OK.
   A went   (B) had   C stayed
2. Last summer we _____ to the beach every day. It was a great holiday.
   A went   B had   C stayed
3. If you visit Madrid you can _____ in my sister's apartment. She's in the UK at the moment.
   A go   B have   C stay
4. We visited a radio station with my school. We _____ a great time. I'd like to be a DJ when I'm older.
   A went   B had   C stayed
5. Do you ever _____ camping? I know a great campsite near the beach.
   A go   B have   C stay
6. Where are you _____ on holiday this year? We're going to Mexico.
   A going   B having   C staying
7. We were _____ a barbecue at the campsite when it started to rain. We all got very wet!
   A going   B having   C staying
8. I'm _____ to a music festival at the weekend. Do you want to come?
   A going   B having   C staying

4 Complete the advert with these words.

campsite   cleaners   ~~earn~~   for   hard   part

JOBS FOR THE SUMMER

Do you want to 1) _earn_ some holiday money? Are you looking 2) _____ a job where you can meet other young people? Then come and work at Joe's 3) _____! You will be 4) _____ of a great team of people who work 5) _____ and have fun. We are looking for waiters and waitresses, 6) _____ and kitchen assistants.

For more information call Joe on 07778826374.

86 GOLD EXPERIENCE

Revision Units 11 – 12

GRAMMAR

1 Choose the correct words.

1. My sister is interested in *to become/becoming* a police officer when she's older.
2. Mark wants *to earn/earning* lots of money and have a fast car.
3. We're looking forward to *starting/start* our summer job at the campsite.
4. Kiera really enjoys *to be/being* with children. She should be a teacher.
5. I've agreed *helping/to help* my aunt and uncle at their restaurant at weekends.
6. Robert is very good at *to fix/fixing* engines. Maybe one day he'll be a mechanic.
7. Emma forgot *switching/to switch* the lights off in the office.
8. Joe and Clare are trying *to find/finding* a Saturday job.

2 Make zero or first conditional sentences. Use the correct form of the verbs in brackets and use contractions where possible.

A: What are we doing on Saturday?

If the weather 1) *is* (be) nice, we 2) _____ (have) a barbecue in the garden.

B: Going on holiday is so expensive!

It 3) _____ (not be) very expensive if you 4) _____ (stay) on a campsite.

C: Which bands are playing at the music festival and how much are tickets?

If you 5) _____ (give) me your email address, I 6) _____ (send) you some information.

3 Complete the sentences with the present passive form of the verbs in brackets.

1. The offices *are cleaned* (clean) every afternoon.
2. You _____ (give) a uniform before you start the job.
3. The job _____ (advertise) on the Internet.
4. Emma _____ (not allow) to wear trainers at work.
5. Robots _____ (use) in my dad's factory.
6. The menu _____ (write) on a blackboard outside the café.

4 Choose the correct words.

1. If we *'ll stay/stay* in Rome, we'll visit the Colosseum.
2. You won't get burnt if you *'ll wear/wear* sun cream.
3. If you like camping, you *borrowed/could borrow* my tent.
4. If Jon and Rosie *will go/go* to Greece in July, it will be very hot.
5. I'll bring my swimsuit if we *go/'ll go* to the beach.
6. James won't go on the school trip if he *doesn't get/won't get* a passport.

Exam information

The *Cambridge English Key for Schools exam* is made up of three papers, each testing a different area of ability in English. The Reading and Writing paper is worth 50 per cent of the marks (60 marks); the Listening paper is worth 25 per cent (25 marks) and the Speaking component is worth 25 per cent. There are five grades. A, B and C are pass grades; D and E are fail grades.

Reading and Writing (1 hour 10 minutes)

Part 1 Matching	Focus	Reading short texts for the main message
	Task	You match five sentences to eight notices.
Part 2 Three-option multiple choice sentences	Focus	Reading and identifying appropriate vocabulary
	Task	You read five sentences on a related topic and select the correct answer.
Part 3 Three-option multiple choice and matching	Focus	Functional language. Identifying an appropriate response
	Task	You match five items in a dialogue, selecting from eight possible responses.
Part 4 Right/wrong/doesn't say or three-option multiple choice	Focus	Reading for detailed understanding and main idea(s)
	Task	You read one long text or three short texts and select the correct answer.
Part 5 Three-option multiple choice cloze	Focus	Reading and identifying appropriate structural words
	Task	You read a text with eight gaps and select the best word to complete each gap.
Part 6 Word completion	Focus	Identifying appropriate word and spelling
	Task	You complete the spelling of five words, using a definition.
Part 7 Open cloze	Focus	Reading and identifying appropriate word
	Task	You read a short text with ten gaps, completing the text with one word in each gap.
Part 8 Information transfer	Focus	Reading with focus on content and accuracy
	Task	You read two short texts to prompt completion of a third text with five gaps (with words or numbers).
Part 9 Guided writing	Focus	Writing a short note, email or postcard of 25–35 words
	Task	You read a short text or rubric to prompt a written response. Three messages to communicate.

Listening (approximately 30 minutes)

Part 1 Three-option multiple choice	Focus	Listening to identify key information
	Task	You listen to five short dialogues and choose the correct picture for each answer.
Part 2 Matching	Focus	Listening to identify key information
	Task	You listen to a longer dialogue and match five items with eight options.
Part 3 Three-option multiple choice	Focus	Listening to identify key information
	Task	You listen to a longer dialogue and choose the correct answer for five items.
Part 4 Gap-fill	Focus	Listening and writing down information
	Task	You listen to a longer dialogue and write the missing word(s) or number in five gaps.
Part 5 Gap-fill	Focus	Listening and writing down information
	Task	You listen to a longer dialogue and write the missing word(s) or number in five gaps.

Speaking (approximately 8–10 minutes)

Part 1 Examiner-led conversation (5–6 minutes)	Focus	Giving personal information
	Task	You answer general questions that the examiner asks.
Part 2 Two-way conversation with visual and written prompt (4 minutes)	Focus	Giving factual information related to daily life
	Task	You ask and answer questions with another candidate using prompt material.

NOTES

NOTES

NOTES

NOTES

NOTES

NOTES

Pearson Education Limited
Edinburgh Gate
Harlow
Essex CM20 2JE
England
and Associated Companies throughout the world.

www.english.com/goldxp

© Pearson Education Limited 2016

The right of Kathryn Alevizos to be identified as author of this Work has been asserted by her in accordance with the Copyright, Designs and Patents Act 1988.

All rights reserved; no part of this publication may be reproduced, stored in a retrieval system, or transmitted in any form or by any means, electronic, mechanical, photocopying, recording, or otherwise without the prior written permission of the Publishers.

First published 2016
Second impression 2019

ISBN: 9781292159461

Set in 10pt Mixage ITC Std
Printed in China

The publisher would like to thank the following for their kind permission to reproduce their photographs:

(Key: b-bottom; c-centre; l-left; r-right; t-top)

123RF.com: 43b, 51 (3), 55cl, 71t, 86, scanrail 69c; **Alamy Images:** Alvey & Towers Picture Library 45, C-images 42tr, doughoughton 39cr, geogphotos 39tr, Germany 39bl, imac 47 (1), Justin Kase z12z 42br, Mar Photographics 47tr (2); **Corbis:** moodboard 47cl (3); **Digital Vision:** 21b; **Fotolia.com:** bloomua 25t (1), chrisdorney 25b (5), Brian Jackson 25 (2), -Marcus- 51 (F), Susan Montgomery 51 (B), photog45 39cl, Flavijus Piliponis 51 (2), pixelrobot 51 (4), Rbut 87, Sinidex 51 (D), Andrew Tobin 51 (E), vbez 51 (C); **Getty Images:** American Idol 2012 / FOX 63, Photographer's Choice 40, Purestock 49, Roy Rainford / Robert Harding 56, X Factor / Ray Mickshaw / Fox 62; **Imagestate Media:** Phovoir 53; **Pearson Education Ltd:** Gareth Boden 19; **PhotoDisc:** C Squared Studios 70, Life File / Andrew Ward 36; **Shutterstock.com:** 2bears 43t, 55b, AJP 71b, Andresr 31, Antonio Guillem 71c, Artazum and Iriana Shiyan 14, Auremar 5, Bakalusha 13, Kenneth William Caleno 51 (1), Catalin Petolea 22b, Centurion Studio 42tl, CREATISTA 79br, dwphotos 65, Elena Elisseeva 42bl, Eric Isselee 37, Evangelos 42cl, Feng Yu 25 (3), Jan Kranendonk 57, Jill Lang 83br, JNP 79bc, Deborah Kolb 35, L i g h t p o e t 21t, Leigh Prather 10, Lilac Mountain 39br, Lilu2005 48, Mangostock 79bl, Margot Petrowski 7, Markus Gann 23, Mihai Simonia 64, Monkey Business Images 38, MSPhotographic 69b, Pavel L Photo and Video 76, Sabphoto 9b, Taina Sohlman 39tl, Stanislav Tiplyashin 67, Stephen Bonk 77, Steve Bower 83bl, Steve Silver Smith 9t, tankist276 47cr (4), Tupungato 25 (4), Viki2win 8, wheatley 41, withGod 74; **SuperStock:** Cultura Limited 47br (6), Ian Murray / Loop Images 33, Tetra Images 47 (5), Travelshots 84

Illustrated by: Clive Goodyer (Beehive Illustration) 47, 68; Caron Painter (Sylvie Poggio) 28; Niall Harding (Beehive Illustration) 8, 15, 24, 27, 37, 50; Simon Stephenson (NB Illustration) 4, 66; Ned Woodman 10, 19, 75

Cover images: *Front:* **Shutterstock.com:** Petrenko Andriy

All other images © Pearson Education

Every effort has been made to trace the copyright holders and we apologise in advance for any unintentional omissions. We would be pleased to insert the appropriate acknowledgement in any subsequent edition of this publication.